UNCLE TOM'S CABIN

Harriet Beecher Stowe

EDITORIAL DIRECTOR Laurie Barnett
DIRECTOR OF TECHNOLOGY Tammy Hepps

SERIES EDITOR John Crowther
MANAGING EDITOR Vincent Janoski

WRITERS Amanda David, Brian Phillips
EDITORS Patrick Flanagan, Katie Mannheimer

This edition published by Spark Publishing

Spark Publishing
A Division of SparkNotes LLC
120 Fifth Avenue, 8th Floor
New York, NY 10011

Any book purchased without a cover is stolen property, reported as "unsold and
destroyed" to the Publisher, who receives no payment for such "stripped books."

Please submit all comments and questions or report errors to www.sparknotes.com/errors

Printed and bound in the United States

ISBN 1-58663-417-8

INTRODUCTION: STOPPING TO BUY SPARKNOTES ON A SNOWY EVENING

Whose words these are you *think* you know.
Your paper's due tomorrow, though;
We're glad to see you stopping here
To get some help before you go.

Lost your course? You'll find it here.
Face tests and essays without fear.
Between the words, good grades at stake:
Get great results throughout the year.

Once school bells caused your heart to quake
As teachers circled each mistake.
Use SparkNotes and no longer weep,
Ace every single test you take.

Yes, books are lovely, dark, and deep,
But only what you grasp you keep,
With hours to go before you sleep,
With hours to go before you sleep.

CONTENTS

CONTEXT

UPON MEETING HARRIET BEECHER STOWE for the first time, Abraham Lincoln reportedly said, "So this is the little lady who made this big war." Stowe was little—under five feet tall—but what she lacked in height, she made up for in influence and success. *Uncle Tom's Cabin* became one of the most widely read and deeply penetrating books of its time. It sold hundreds of thousands of copies and was translated into numerous languages. Many historians have credited the novel with contributing to the outbreak of the Civil War.

The daughter of an eminent New England preacher, Stowe was born into a family of eccentric, intelligent people. As a child, she learned Latin and wrote a children's geography book, both before she was ten years old. Throughout her life, she remained deeply involved in religious movements, feminist causes, and the most divisive political and moral issue of her time: the abolition of slavery.

Stowe grew up in the Northeast but lived for a time in Cincinnati, which enabled her to see both sides of the slavery debate without losing her abolitionist's perspective. Cincinnati was evenly split for and against abolition, and Stowe wrote satirical pieces on the subject for several local papers there. She often wrote pieces under pseudonyms and with contrasting styles, and one can see a similar attention to voice in *Uncle Tom's Cabin*, in which dialects and patterns of speech contrast among characters. Though Stowe absorbed a great deal of information about slavery during her Cincinnati years, she nonetheless conducted extensive research before writing *Uncle Tom's Cabin*. She wrote to Frederick Douglass and others for help in creating a realistic picture of slavery in the Deep South. Her black cook and household servants also helped by telling her stories of their slave days.

Stowe's main goal with *Uncle Tom's Cabin* was to convince her large Northern readership of the necessity of ending slavery. Most immediately, the novel served as a response to the passage of the Fugitive Slave Act of 1850, which made it illegal to give aid or assistance to a runaway slave. Under this legislation, Southern slaves who escaped to the North had to flee to Canada in order to find real freedom. With her book, Stowe created a sort of exposé that revealed the horrors of Southern slavery to people in the North. Her radical position on race relations, though, was informed by a deep religiosity. Stowe continually emphasizes the importance of Christian love in eradicating oppression. She also works in her feminist beliefs, showing women as equals to men in intelligence, bravery, and spiritual strength. Indeed, women dominate the book's moral code, proving vital advisors to their husbands, who often need help in seeing through convention and popular opinion.

Uncle Tom's Cabin was published in episodes in the *National Era* in 1851 and 1852, then published in its entirety on March 20, 1852. It sold 10,000 copies in its first week and 300,000 by the end of the year, astronomical numbers for the mid-nineteenth century. Today, analysis of both the book's conception and reception proves helpful in our understanding of the Civil War era. Within the text itself, the reader finds insights into the mind of a Christian, feminist abolitionist. For example, in the arguments Stowe uses, the reader receives a glimpse into the details of the slavery debate. Looking beyond the text to its impact on its society, the reader gains an understanding of the historical forces contributing to the outbreak of war.

PLOT OVERVIEW

HAVING RUN UP LARGE DEBTS, a Kentucky farmer named Arthur Shelby faces the prospect of losing everything he owns. Though he and his wife, Emily Shelby, have a kindhearted and affectionate relationship with their slaves, Shelby decides to raise money by selling two of his slaves to Mr. Haley, a coarse slave trader. The slaves in question are Uncle Tom, a middle-aged man with a wife and children on the farm, and Harry, the young son of Mrs. Shelby's maid Eliza. When Shelby tells his wife about his agreement with Haley, she is appalled because she has promised Eliza that Shelby would not sell her son.

However, Eliza overhears the conversation between Haley and his wife and, after warning Uncle Tom and his wife, Aunt Chloe, she takes Harry and flees to the North, hoping to find freedom with her husband George in Canada. Haley pursues her, but two other Shelby slaves alert Eliza to the danger. She miraculously evades capture by crossing the half-frozen Ohio River, the boundary separating Kentucky from the North. Haley hires a slave hunter named Loker and his gang to bring Eliza and Harry back to Kentucky. Eliza and Harry make their way to a Quaker settlement, where the Quakers agree to help transport them to safety. They are joined at the settlement by George, who reunites joyously with his family for the trip to Canada.

Meanwhile, Uncle Tom sadly leaves his family and Mas'r George, Shelby's young son and Tom's friend, as Haley takes him to a boat on the Mississippi to be transported to a slave market. On the boat, Tom meets an angelic little white girl named Eva, who quickly befriends him. When Eva falls into the river, Tom dives in to save her, and her father, Augustine St. Clare, gratefully agrees to buy Tom from Haley. Tom travels with the St. Clares to their home in New Orleans, where he grows increasingly invaluable to the St. Clare household and increasingly close to Eva, with whom he shares a devout Christianity.

Up North, George and Eliza remain in flight from Loker and his men. When Loker attempts to capture them, George shoots him in the side, and the other slave hunters retreat. Eliza convinces George and the Quakers to bring Loker to the next settlement, where he can be healed. Meanwhile, in New Orleans, St. Clare discusses slavery with his cousin Ophelia, who opposes slavery as an institution but harbors deep prejudices against blacks. St. Clare, by contrast, feels no hostility against blacks but tolerates slavery because he feels powerless to change it. To help Ophelia overcome her bigotry, he buys Topsy, a young black girl who was abused by her past master and arranges for Ophelia to begin educating her.

After Tom has lived with the St. Clares for two years, Eva grows very ill. She slowly weakens, then dies, with a vision of heaven before her. Her death has a profound effect on everyone who knew her: Ophelia resolves to love the slaves, Topsy learns to trust and feel attached to others, and St. Clare decides to set Tom free. However, before he can act on his decision, St. Clare is stabbed to death while trying to settle a brawl. As he dies, he at last finds God and goes to be reunited with his mother in heaven.

St. Clare's cruel wife, Marie, sells Tom to a vicious plantation owner named Simon Legree. Tom is taken to rural Louisiana with a group of new slaves, including Emmeline, whom the demonic Legree has purchased to use as a sex slave, replacing his previous sex slave Cassy. Legree takes a strong dislike to Tom when Tom refuses to whip a fellow slave as ordered. Tom receives a severe beating, and Legree resolves to crush his faith in God. Tom meets Cassy, and hears her story. Separated from her daughter by slavery, she became pregnant again but killed the child because she could not stand to have another child taken from her.

Around this time, with the help of Tom Loker—now a changed man after being healed by the Quakers—George, Eliza, and Harry at last cross over into Canada from Lake Erie and obtain their freedom. In Louisiana, Tom's faith is sorely tested by his hardships, and he nearly ceases to believe. He has two visions, however—one of Christ and one of Eva—which renew his spiritual strength and give him the courage to withstand Legree's torments. He encourages Cassy to escape. She does so, taking Emmeline with her, after she devises a ruse in which she and Emmeline pretend to be ghosts. When Tom refuses to tell Legree where Cassy and Emmeline have gone, Legree orders his overseers to beat him. When Tom is near death, he forgives Legree and the overseers. George Shelby arrives with money in hand to buy Tom's freedom, but he is too late. He can only watch as Tom dies a martyr's death.

Taking a boat toward freedom, Cassy and Emmeline meet George Harris's sister and travel with her to Canada, where Cassy realizes that Eliza is her long-lost daughter. The newly reunited family travels to France and decides to move to Liberia, the African nation created for former American slaves. George Shelby returns to the Kentucky farm, where, after his father's death, he sets all the slaves free in honor of Tom's memory. He urges them to think on Tom's sacrifice every time they look at his cabin and to lead a pious Christian life, just as Tom did.

CHARACTER LIST

Uncle Tom A good and pious man, Uncle Tom is the protagonist of *Uncle Tom's Cabin*. Even under the worst conditions, Uncle Tom always prays to God and finds a way to keep his faith. As the novel progresses, the cruel treatment that Tom suffers at the hands of Simon Legree threatens his belief in God, but Tom withstands his doubts and dies the death of a Christian martyr.

Aunt Chloe Uncle Tom's wife and the Shelbys' cook. Chloe often acts like a jovial simpleton around the Shelbys to mask her more complex feelings.

Arthur Shelby The owner of Uncle Tom in Kentucky, Shelby sells Tom to the cruel Mr. Haley to pay off his debts. An educated, kind, and basically good-hearted man, Shelby nonetheless tolerates and perpetuates slavery. Stowe uses him to illustrate that the immorality inherent in slavery makes villains of all its practitioners—not just the most cruel masters.

Emily Shelby Mr. Shelby's wife, Emily Shelby is a loving, Christian woman who does not believe in slavery. She uses her influence with her husband to try to help the Shelbys' slaves and is one of the novel's many morally virtuous and insightful female characters.

George Shelby Called "Mas'r George" by Uncle Tom, George is the Shelbys' good-hearted son. He loves Tom and promises to rescue him from the cruelty into which his father sold him. After Tom dies, he resolves to free all the slaves on the family farm in Kentucky. More morally committed than his father, George not only possesses a kind heart but acts on his principles.

George Harris Eliza's husband and an intellectually curious and talented mulatto, George loves his family deeply and willingly fights for his freedom. He confronts the slave hunter Tom Loker and does not hesitate to shoot him when he imperils the family.

Eliza Harris Mrs. Shelby's maid, George's wife, and Harry's mother, Eliza is an intelligent, beautiful, and brave young slave. After Mr. Shelby makes known his plans to sell Eliza's son to Mr. Haley, she proves the force of her motherly love as well as her strength of spirit by making a spectacular escape. Her crossing of the Ohio River on patches of ice is the novel's most famous scene.

Harry Harris Eliza and George's son, a young boy.

Augustine St. Clare Tom's master in New Orleans and Eva's father, St. Clare is a flighty and romantic man, dedicated to pleasure. St. Clare does not believe in God, and he carouses and drinks every night. Although he dotes on his daughter and treats his slaves with compassion, St. Clare shares the hypocrisy of Mr. Shelby in that he sees the evil of slavery but nonetheless tolerates and practices it.

Eva St. Clare and Marie's angelic daughter. Eva, also referred to in the book as Little Eva (her given name is Evangeline) is presented as an absolutely perfect child—a completely moral being and an unimpeachable Christian. She laments the existence of slavery and sees no difference between blacks and whites. After befriending Tom while still a young girl, Eva becomes one of the most important figures in his life. In death, Eva becomes one of the text's central Christ figures.

Miss Ophelia St. Clare's cousin from the North (Vermont) who comes to help him manage the household, Ophelia opposes slavery in the abstract. However, she finds actual slaves somewhat distasteful and harbors considerable prejudice against them. After Eva's death, and through her relationship with Topsy, Ophelia realizes her failings and learns to see slaves as human beings. Stowe hoped that much of her Northern audience might recognize themselves in Ophelia and reconsider their views on slavery.

Marie   St. Clare's wife, a self-centered woman. Petty, whining, and foolish, she is the very opposite of the idealized woman figure that appears repeatedly throughout the novel.

The Quakers The Quakers, a Christian group that arose in mid-seventeenth-century England, dedicated themselves to achieving an inner understanding of God, without the use of creeds, clergy, or outward rites. The Quakers have a long history of contributing to social reform and peace efforts. In *Uncle Tom's Cabin*, many Quaker characters appear who help George and Eliza, as well as many other slaves. Stowe uses them to portray a Christianity free of hypocrisy, self-righteous display, or bigoted conventions. This kind of Christianity, she implies, can play a crucial role in the abolition of slavery.

Senator and Mrs. Bird Mrs. Bird is another example of the virtuous woman. She tries to exert influence through her husband. Senator Bird exemplifies the well-meaning man who is sympathetic to the abolitionist cause but who nonetheless remains complacent or resigned to the status quo.

Tom Loker A slave hunter hired by Mr. Haley to bring back Eliza, Harry, and George, Tom Loker first appears as a gruff, violent man. George shoots him when he tries to capture them, and, after he is healed by the Quakers, Loker experiences a transformation and chooses to join the Quakers rather than return to his old life.

Mr. Haley The slave trader who buys Uncle Tom and Harry from Mr. Shelby. A gruff, coarse man, Haley presents himself as a kind individual who treats his slaves well. Haley, however, mistreats his slaves, often violently.

Topsy A wild and uncivilized slave girl whom Miss Ophelia tries to reform, Topsy gradually learns to love and respect others by following the example of Eva.

Simon Legree Tom's ruthlessly evil master on the Louisiana plantation. A vicious, barbaric, and loathsome man, Legree fosters violence and hatred among his slaves.

Cassy Legree's (slave) mistress and Eliza's mother, Cassy proves a proud and intelligent woman and devises a clever way to escape Legree's plantation.

Emmeline A young and beautiful slave girl whom Legree buys for himself, perhaps to replace Cassy as his mistress. She has been raised as a pious Christian.

CHARACTER LIST

ANALYSIS OF MAJOR CHARACTERS

UNCLE TOM

History has not been kind to Uncle Tom, the hero of *Uncle Tom's Cabin* and one of the most popular figures of nineteenth-century American fiction. After its initial burst of sensational popularity and influence, *Uncle Tom's Cabin* fell into neglect. Its circulation declined following the end of the Civil War and Stowe's death, and by the mid-1900s, the book was virtually out of print. Not until the early 1960s, when the Civil Rights Movement reawakened an interest in anti-slavery fiction, did the novel again become widely read. More than a hundred years after its initial publication, however, *Uncle Tom's Cabin* stood as a testament to a past set of standards and expectations. The values and attributes that seemed admirable in its characters in 1852 frequently appeared incomprehensible and even contemptible to twentieth-century readers. In particular, the passive acceptance of slavery practiced by the novel's title character seemed horrendously out of line with the resolve and strength of modern black Civil Rights crusaders. The term "Uncle Tom" became an insult, conjuring an image of an old black man eager to please his white masters and happy to accept his own position of inferiority.

Although modern readers' criticisms hold some validity, the notion of an "Uncle Tom" contains generalizations not found within the actual character in the novel. First, Tom is not an old man. The novel states that he is eight years older than Shelby, which probably places him in his late forties at the start of the novel. Moreover, Tom does not accept his position of inferiority with happiness. Tom's passivity owes not to stupidity or to contentment with his position, but to his deep religious values, which impel him to love everyone and selflessly endure his trials. Indeed, Tom's central characteristic in the novel is this religiosity, his strength of faith. Everywhere Tom goes in the novel, he manages to spread some of the love and goodwill of his religious beliefs, helping to alleviate the pain of slavery and enhance the hope of salvation. And while this religiosity translates into a selfless passivity on Tom's part, it also translates into a policy of warm encouragement of others' attempts at freedom. Thus, he supports Eliza's escape, as well as that of Cassy and Emmeline from the Legree plantation. Moreover, while Tom may not actively seek his own freedom, he practices a kind of resistance in his passivity. When Legree orders him to beat the slave girl in Chapter XXXIII, he refuses, standing firm in his values. He will submit to being beaten for his beliefs, but he will not capitulate or run away.

Moreover, even in recognizing Tom's passivity in the novel, and Stowe's approving treatment of it, one should note that Stowe does not present this behavior as a model of *black* behavior, but as a heroic model of behavior that should be practiced by everyone, black and white. Stowe makes it very clear that if the villainous white slaveholders of the novel were to achieve Tom's selfless Christian love for others, slavery would be impossible, and Tom's death never would have happened. Because Stowe believes that a transformation through Christian love must occur before slavery can be abolished successfully, she holds up Tom's death as nobler than any escape, in that it provides an example for others and offers the hope of a more generalized salvation. Through this death, moreover, Tom becomes a Christ figure, a radical role for a black character to play in American fiction in 1852. Tom's death proves Legree's fundamental moral and personal inferiority, and provides the motivating force behind George Shelby's decision to free all the slaves. By practicing selflessness and loving his enemy, Tom becomes a martyr and affects social change. Although contemporary society finds its heroes in active agents of social change and tends to discourage submissiveness, Stowe meant for Tom to embody noble heroic tendencies of his own. She portrayed his passivity as a virtue unconnected to his minority status. Within the world of *Uncle Tom's Cabin*, Tom is presented as more than a black hero—he is presented as a hero transcending race.

OPHELIA ST. CLARE

Probably the most complex female character in the novel, Ophelia deserves special attention from the reader because she is treated as a surrogate for Stowe's intended audience. It is as if Stowe conceived an imaginary picture of her intended reader, then brought that reader into the book as a character. Ophelia embodies what Stowe considered a widespread Northern problem: the white person who opposes slavery on a theoretical level but feels racial prejudice and hatred in the presence of an actual black slave. Ophelia detests slavery, but she considers it almost necessary for blacks, against whom she harbors a deep-seated prejudice—she does not want them to touch her. Stowe emphasizes that much of Ophelia's racial prejudice stems from unfamiliarity and ignorance rather than from actual experience-based hatred. Because Ophelia has seldom spent time in the presence of slaves, she finds them uncomfortably alien.

However, Ophelia is one of the only characters in *Uncle Tom's Cabin* who develops as the story progresses. Once St. Clare puts Topsy in her care, Ophelia begins to have increased contact with a slave. At first she tries to teach Topsy out of a sense of mere duty. But Stowe suggests that duty alone will not eradicate slavery—abolitionists must act out of love. Eva's death proves the crucial catalyst in Ophelia's transformation, and she comes to love Topsy as a human being, overcoming her racial prejudice and offering a model to Stowe's Northern readers.

SIMON LEGREE

Although largely a uniformly evil villain, Simon Legree does possess some psychological depth as a character. He has been deeply affected by the death of his angelic mother and seems to show some legitimate affection for Cassy. Nonetheless, Legree's main purpose in the book is as a foil to Uncle Tom, and as an effective picture of slavery at its worst. Often associated with firelight and flames, Legree demonstrates literally infernal qualities, and his devilishness provides an effective contrast with the angelic qualities of his passive slave. Legree's demoniacally evil ways also play an important role in shaping the end of the book along the lines of the traditional Christian narrative. Above all, Legree desires to break Tom's religious faith and to see him capitulate to doubt and sin. In the end, although Tom dies and Legree survives, the evil that Legree stands for has been destroyed. Tom dies loving the men who kill him, proving that his faith prevails over Legree's evil.

THEMES, MOTIFS & SYMBOLS

THEMES

Themes are the fundamental and often universal ideas explored in a literary work.

THE EVIL OF SLAVERY

Uncle Tom's Cabin was written after the passage of the Fugitive Slave Act of 1850, which made it illegal for anyone in the United States to offer aid or assistance to a runaway slave. The novel seeks to attack this law and the institution it protected, ceaselessly advocating the immediate emancipation of the slaves and freedom for all people. Each of Stowe's scenes, while serving to further character and plot, also serves, without exception, to persuade the reader—especially the Northern reader of Stowe's time—that slavery is evil, un-Christian, and intolerable in a civil society.

For most of the novel, Stowe explores the question of slavery in a fairly mild setting, in which slaves and masters have seemingly positive relationships. At the Shelbys' house, and again at the St. Clares', the slaves have kindly masters who do not abuse or mistreat them. Stowe does not offer these settings in order to show slavery's evil as conditional. She seeks to expose the vices of slavery even in its best-case scenario. Though Shelby and St. Clare possess kindness and intelligence, their ability to tolerate slavery renders them hypocritical and morally weak. Even under kind masters, slaves suffer, as we see when a financially struggling Shelby guiltily destroys Tom's family by selling Tom, and when the fiercely selfish Marie, by demanding attention be given to herself, prevents the St. Clare slaves from mourning the death of her own angelic daughter, Eva. A common contemporary defense of slavery claimed that the institution benefited the slaves because most masters acted in their slaves' best interest. Stowe refutes this argument with her biting portrayals, insisting that the slave's best interest can lie only in obtaining freedom.

In the final third of the book, Stowe leaves behind the pleasant veneer of life at the Shelby and St. Clare houses and takes her reader into the Legree plantation, where the evil of slavery appears in its most naked and hideous form. This harsh and barbaric setting, in which slaves suffer beatings, sexual abuse, and even murder, introduces the power of shock into Stowe's argument. If slavery is wrong in the best of cases, in the worst of cases it is nightmarish and inhuman. In the book's structural progression between "pleasant" and hellish plantations, we can detect Stowe's rhetorical methods. First she deflates the defense of the pro-slavery reader by showing the evil of the "best" kind of slavery. She then presents her own case against slavery by showing the shocking wickedness of slavery at its worst.

THE INCOMPATIBILITY OF SLAVERY & CHRISTIAN VALUES

Writing for a predominantly religious, predominantly Protestant audience, Stowe takes great pains to illustrate the fact that the system of slavery and the moral code of Christianity oppose each other. No Christian, she insists, should be able to tolerate slavery. Throughout the novel, the more religious a character is, the more he or she objects to slavery. Eva, the most morally perfect white character in the novel, fails to understand why anyone would see a difference between blacks and whites. In contrast, the morally revolting, nonreligious Legree practices slavery almost as a policy of deliberate blasphemy and evil. Christianity, in Stowe's novel, rests on a principle of universal love. If all people were to put this principle into practice, Stowe insists, it would be impossible for one segment of humanity to oppress and enslave another. Thus, not only are Christianity and slavery incompatible, but Christianity can actually be used to fight slavery.

The slave hunter Tom Loker learns this lesson after his life is spared by the slaves he tried to capture, and after being healed by the generous-hearted and deeply religious Quakers. He becomes a changed man. Moreover, Uncle Tom ultimately triumphs over slavery in his adherence to Christ's command to "love thine enemy." He refuses to compromise his Christian faith in the face of the many trials he undergoes at Legree's plantation. When he is beaten to death by Legree and his men, he dies forgiving them. In this way, Tom becomes a Christian martyr, a model for the behavior of both whites and blacks. The story of his life both exposes the evil of slavery—its incompatibility with Christian virtue—and points the way to its transformation through Christian love.

The Moral Power of Women

Although Stowe wrote *Uncle Tom's Cabin* before the widespread growth of the women's rights movement of the late 1800s, the reader can nevertheless regard the book as a specimen of early feminism. The text portrays women as morally conscientious, committed, and courageous—indeed, often as *more* morally conscientious, committed, and courageous than men. Stowe implies a parallel between the oppression of blacks and the oppression of women, yet she expresses hope for the oppressed in her presentation of women as effectively influencing their husbands. Moreover, she shows how this show of strength by one oppressed group can help to alleviate the oppression of the other. White women can use their influence to convince their husbands—the people with voting rights—of the evil of slavery.

Throughout the novel, the reader sees many examples of idealized womanhood, of perfect mothers and wives who attempt to find salvation for their morally inferior husbands or sons. Examples include Mrs. Bird, St. Clare's mother, Legree's mother, and, to a lesser extent, Mrs. Shelby. The text also portrays black women in a very positive light. Black women generally prove strong, brave, and capable, as seen especially in the character of Eliza. In the cases where women do not act morally—such as Prue in her drunkenness or Cassy with her infanticide, the women's sins are presented as illustrating slavery's evil influence rather than the women's own immorality. Not all women appear as bolsters to the book's moral code: Marie acts petty and mean, and Ophelia begins the novel with many prejudices. Nonetheless, the book seems to argue the existence of a natural female sense of good and evil, pointing to an inherent moral wisdom in the gender as a whole and encouraging the use of this wisdom as a force for social change.

Motifs

Motifs are recurring structures, contrasts, or literary devices that can help to develop and inform the text's major themes.

Christ Figures

As befits its religious preoccupation, the novel presents two instances of a sacrificial death linked to Christ's. Eva and Tom, the two most morally perfect characters in the novel, both die in atmospheres of charged religious belief, and both die, in a sense, to achieve salvation for others. Eva's death leads to St. Clare's deathbed

conversion to Christianity and to Ophelia's recognition and denuncia-
tion of her own racial prejudice. Tom's death leads to Emmeline and
Cassy's escape and to the freedom of all the slaves on the Shelby farm in
Kentucky. Both Tom and Eva are explicitly compared to Christ:
Ophelia says that Eva resembles Jesus, and the narrator depicts Tom
carrying his cross behind Jesus. This motif of Christ-like sacrifice and
death enables Stowe to underscore her basic point about Christian
goodness while holding up models of moral perfection for her reader to
emulate. It also enables her to create the emotionally charged, sentimental death scenes popular in nineteenth-century literature.

THE SUPERNATURAL
Several supernatural instances of divine intervention in the novel
suggest that a higher order exists to oppose slavery. For instance,
when Eliza leaps over the Ohio river, jumping rapidly between
blocks of ice without fear or pain, the text tells us that she has been
endowed with a "strength such as God gives only to the desperate,"
facilitating her escape from oppression. Similarly, when Tom's faith
begins to lapse at the Legree plantation, he is visited by religious visions
that restore it, thus sustaining him in his passive resistance of Legree.
Before Eva dies, she glimpses a view of heaven and experiences a miraculous presentiment of her own death; these occurrences reinforce Eva's
purity and add moral authority to her anti-slavery stance.

Instances of supernaturalism thus support various characters in
their efforts to resist or fight slavery. But they also serve to thwart
other characters in their efforts to practice slavery. Thus, as Legree
pursues his oppression of Tom, he has an upsetting vision of his
dead mother and becomes temporarily paralyzed by an apparition
of a ghost in the fog. The fear caused by this apparition weakens Legree to the point that Cassy and Emmeline can trick him into believing
that ghosts haunt the garret. This ploy enables them to escape.

SYMBOLS

---

*Symbols are objects, characters, figures, or colors used to
represent abstract ideas or concepts.*

UNCLE TOM'S CABIN
Near the end of the book, after George Shelby frees his slaves, he
tells them that, when they look at Uncle Tom's cabin, they should
remember their freedom and dedicate themselves to leading a Chris-

tian life like Uncle Tom's. The sight of Uncle Tom's cabin on George Shelby's property serves as a persistent reminder to him of the sufferings Tom experienced as a slave. The cabin also becomes a metaphor for Uncle Tom's willingness to be beaten and even killed rather than harm or betray his fellow slaves—his willingness to suffer and die rather than go against Christian values of love and loyalty. The image of the cabin thus neatly encapsulates the main themes of the book, signifying both the destructive power of slavery and the ability of Christian love to overcome it.

ELIZA'S LEAP
The scene of Eliza's leap across the half-frozen Ohio river constitutes the most famous episode in *Uncle Tom's Cabin*. The scene also serves as an important metaphor. The leap from the southern to the northern bank of the river symbolizes in one dramatic moment the process of leaving slavery for freedom. Indeed, Eliza's leap from one bank to the next literally constitutes a leap from the slave-holding states to the non-slave-holding states, as the Ohio River served as the legally recognized divide between South and North. The dangers Eliza faces in her leap, and the courage she requires to execute it successfully, represent the more general instances of peril and heroism involved in any slave's journey to freedom.

GEOGRAPHY
Uncle Tom's Cabin uses the North to represent freedom and the South to represent slavery and oppression. Obviously the opposition is rooted in history. However, Stowe embellishes the opposition so as to transform it from literal to literary. Two main stories dominate the novel—the story of Eliza and George and the story of Uncle Tom. One story serves as an escape narrative, chronicling Eliza and George's flight to freedom. The other story is a slavery narrative, chronicling Uncle Tom's descent into increasingly worse states of oppression. Not surprisingly, the action in the escape narrative moves increasingly northward, with Canada representing its endpoint and the attainment of freedom by the escaped slaves. The action in the slavery narrative moves increasingly southward, with Tom's death occurring on Legree's plantation in rural Louisiana, far into the Deep South. This geographical split represents the wide gulf between freedom and slavery and plays into Stowe's general use of parallelism and contrast in making her political points.

SYMBOLS

Summary & Analysis

Chapters I–V

Summary: Chapter I

On a farm in Kentucky, during a cold February afternoon in the middle of the nineteenth century, two white men sit discussing a business transaction. Arthur Shelby, a gentleman and slaveholder, is negotiating to sell some slaves to Mr. Haley, a coarse slave buyer. Mr. Shelby has fallen into debt and must sell several slaves to raise money, or else he will lose all his land and property. He tells Haley of a fine slave he owns, Uncle Tom—an uncommonly good and honest man, and a devout Christian. Haley says that one slave alone will not suffice, and he asks for Shelby to include a boy or girl with the trade. Despite Shelby's reluctance, they decide upon Harry, the son of Eliza, Mrs. Shelby's maid. Before the trade is finalized, however, Mr. Shelby says he must talk the matter over with his wife. While the men are talking, Eliza approaches Mrs. Shelby and asks her worriedly if Mr. Shelby is going to sell Harry. Mrs. Shelby, uninformed of her husband's financial woes, promises Eliza that Mr. Shelby would never consider such a thing.

Summary: Chapter II

We learn that the beautiful Eliza married a talented mulatto named George, but was separated from him when he was hired out to work in a factory nearby. He invented a machine to speed the process of cleaning hemp, thereby earning the admiration of the factory's proprietor. However, George's master removed him from the factory, saying that he only invented the machine because he was too lazy to work. He put George to work at menial labor, which meant that he could see his wife only infrequently. George and Eliza lost two young children, making Eliza very protective of her only surviving child, Harry.

Summary: Chapter III

George comes to see Eliza soon after her conversation with Mrs. Shelby and tells her that he is going to escape because he can no longer bear the miseries he has been suffering. Eliza urges him to practice Christian restraint and to trust in God, but George explains that his master is urging him to take another woman as his wife. Eliza protests, and George reminds her that there are no lawful marriages among slaves. As he leaves, he tells Eliza that he will head north for Canada in a week; once there, he will work to buy freedom for Eliza and Harry.

SUMMARY: CHAPTER IV
In Uncle Tom's cabin, Aunt Chloe is cooking dinner for Tom and the children. Shelby's son, young Mas'r George, is teaching Tom how to write the letter G. They laugh and talk, bantering about, then eating griddlecakes and discussing pies. After dinner they hold a prayer meeting at which the gathered slaves sing hymns and Mas'r George reads the last chapters of Revelation.

While this happy scene takes place in the cabin, Mr. Shelby agrees to sell both Tom and Harry. He signs the papers, and Mr. Haley relieves him of his mortgage. Shelby reminds Haley that he has promised not to sell Tom to any but the kindest master. Haley states unconvincingly that he will do his best.

SUMMARY: CHAPTER V
That evening, Shelby tells his wife about the sale. Mrs. Shelby, appalled, tries to convince her husband not to sell the slaves—after all, he has promised to set Tom free, and she has promised Eliza that Harry would not be taken away from her. But Mr. Shelby tells her that he must either sell those two slaves, or sell all of his property. Mrs. Shelby declares that slavery is a sin, that she hates slavery and wishes that she could do something to stop it. She offers to sell her watch to save Harry. Shelby apologizes to his wife, but says that the papers are already signed.

Eliza overhears their conversation. Realizing that her son is going to be sold, she takes him, tells him to be quiet, and carries him to Uncle Tom's cabin. There, the prayer meeting has ended, and Eliza tells Tom and Chloe what she has heard. Tom says that he will not try to escape, but Eliza must. Eliza states her intention to head to Canada and asks Tom and Chloe to tell George to look for her. Taking her child, she glides into the night.

ANALYSIS: CHAPTERS I–V
Harriet Beecher Stowe wrote *Uncle Tom's Cabin* with a particular purpose in mind: to educate readers in the North about what was happening in the South. At the time of the book's publication in the early 1850s, the two regions stood so culturally divided that in some

ways they seemed like two separate nations—indeed, the South would try to formalize this during the Civil War—and there was often little communication between them. The novel starts in Kentucky, then progresses into the Deep South. This gradual move southward is designed to give the Northern reader time to become familiar with the foreign world of the South.

Stowe uses relentless irony to expose the moral hypocrisies of the slave trade. The idea of the good slaveholder, as embodied by Shelby, is one such hypocrisy. After guiltily concluding the deal with Haley in Chapter IV, Shelby indulges in a cigar to soothe his nerves. At the same time as he smokes this comforting cigar, two families are being torn apart by his actions. The scenes in Chapter IV, in which we first see a seemingly happy evening in Uncle Tom's cabin, and then see Shelby signing the papers that will destroy Uncle Tom's family, use understatement and contrast to point out the horror of slavery. Elsewhere, Stowe uses biting sarcasm, as when she refers to Haley as a "man of humanity." Stowe mocks contemporary thinkers who claimed the possibility of a "humane" or "benign" slavery. Although Tom and Harry may be comparatively well-off under the ownership of Shelby, Stowe shows how easily a slave can slip from a decent life to an abusive one. Even a relatively kind slaveholder makes no difference in the system. Such a construction, in which one cruel slaveholder can imperil the well-being of any slave, is inherently wrong. Indeed, the institution makes an otherwise decent man into an instrument of cruelty.

Stowe employs a direct and conversational style. She writes to the reader using the pronouns "us" and "you," very conscious of the book's status as her own personal expression of opinion, intended for a specific audience. Before Stowe wrote *Uncle Tom's Cabin*, she wrote parlor literature—long, detailed letters intended to be read out loud before a group. In these texts Stowe would allow her voice to emerge strong and clear. *Uncle Tom's Cabin* was first published in episodes in a newspaper, and took a form similar to these letters.

These first chapters also serve to introduce the main themes of the book. While the book most conspicuously emphasizes the evils of slavery, it also discusses issues of feminism and religion. Mrs. Shelby provides the voice of morality in the conversation between herself and Mr. Shelby in Chapter V, and she plays a similar role throughout the novel; indeed, in general, the novel's women are presented as much more virtuous and pious than its men. Yet Stowe was conscious of her society's reluctance to regard women as equal to men. Therefore, although she uses female characters as gentle sources of prodding to male characters, she never allows them to gain full authority in any situation. Mrs. Shelby influences her husband only through tempered and polite remarks; Stowe may have believed that such techniques were needed in order to avoid alienating the men in her *audience* as well. Nonetheless, Stowe seems to show a deep faith in the power of a woman's influence over a man, whether exerted timidly or more forcefully. In writing her book, Stowe may have been banking on the influence of women to make her text's message fully heard. In many ways, the novel is an appeal to female readers. For instance, Stowe focuses on the relationship between women such as Eliza and their families, demonstrating how slavery breaks these bonds. Stowe may have hoped that her women readers would identify particularly with these wronged women characters, come to believe in the evil of slavery, and then convert their husbands, brothers, fathers, and sons.

CHAPTERS VI–IX

SUMMARY: CHAPTER VI

The next morning, when Mrs. Shelby rings the bell for Eliza, she receives no answer. Realizing what has happened, Mrs. Shelby thanks the Lord. She rejoices that Eliza has fled rather than permitting her child to be taken from her. Mr. Shelby laments the escape, however, fearing that Mr. Haley might think he has helped Eliza to run away in order to avoid selling the boy.

Haley arrives to take Tom and Harry. Hearing from the other slaves that Eliza has run off with her son, he barges into the house, confronting Mr. Shelby with the news. Mr. Shelby asks him to be more polite in Mrs. Shelby's company. The men talk for some moments, Mr. Shelby becoming more and more repulsed by Haley's coarse manners. Finally, Shelby asks several of the slaves to ready a horse for Haley, who intends to ride in pursuit of Eliza. The slaves take as long as possible, and then hide a beechnut under the saddle, in such a way that any weight on the saddle would cause the horse great annoyance. Mrs. Shelby tells Sam, one of the slaves, to show Haley the road and escort him on his way, but cautions not to ride the horses too fast, ostensibly because one of them was recently lame. When Haley sits on his horse, the colt feels the beechnut and throws Haley off, and the whole place erupts into chaos, delaying the man for some time more. By the time the horses are ready again, it is nearly lunchtime. Sam suggests that Haley may need to eat before the journey, and Mrs. Shelby, overhearing, emerges to invite Haley in to dine.

SUMMARY: CHAPTER VII

When Eliza leaves Uncle Tom's cabin, she feels desperate and lonely, and tortured by a maternal sense of panic for her imperiled child. She prays to God and travels throughout the night, finally reaching the Ohio River, the barrier between the South and the North. Springtime ice covers half of the waterway, preventing the river's ferry from running. Eliza learns from the hostess of a bank-side public house that a boatman might attempt a crossing later in the evening. Eliza takes a room at an inn so that her son can sleep. From the window, she gazes out at the river, desperately longing to cross.

Back at Shelby's farm, Aunt Chloe prepares the meal at the most leisurely pace possible, in an attempt to delay the chase. Finally, around two o'clock, the search party embarks. Andy and Sam, two of the younger slaves, serve as Haley's escorts. The young slaves trick Haley into following a route that Eliza would not have taken. Haley is slowed down considerably, but he finally makes it to the town on the river, forty-five minutes after Eliza has laid Harry to sleep in the rented room. Sam sees Eliza standing in the window, and, allowing his hat to be blown off, shouts as if in surprise. With this action, he alerts her to their presence. She throws open the door to her room, which faces the river, grabs Harry, and leaps over the rushing currents onto a raft of ice. She springs from one chunk of ice to the next, oblivious to all pain and cold, until she reaches the other side. A man on the other side helps her up. Eliza recognizes him as Mr. Symmes, the owner of a farm not far from her old home. He fears to offer her shelter himself, but points out a house where she will receive aid.

SUMMARY: CHAPTER VIII

The bewildered Haley cannot follow Eliza across the river and must return to the tavern. There he meets up with Tom Loker, a man who hunts slaves professionally. Haley pays Loker and his partner Marks fifty dollars to hunt down Eliza and Harry. The three men make the following deal: if Loker and Marks catch the slaves, they may take Eliza as long as they bring Harry back to Haley. Meanwhile, Andy and Sam, unaware of this transaction, return to the Shelby house with the joyful story of Eliza's leap.

Summary: Chapter IX

*"...I don't know anything about politics, but I can read
my Bible; and there I see that I must feed the hungry,
clothe the naked, and comfort the desolate."*

(See Quotations, p. 53)

Across the river in Ohio, Senator Bird sits in his house with his wife.
The Ohio State Senate has just passed a law forbidding the assistance of runaway slaves (The Fugitive Slave Law of 1850), and Senator Bird voted in its favor. Mrs. Bird reprimands her husband,
declaring the law immoral and asking Senator Bird if he could truly
turn away a helpless slave if one were to come to him for help. At
that moment, Eliza and Harry arrive at the Birds' doorstep, directed
there by Mr. Symmes, and Senator Bird and his wife bring them into
the house. Senator Bird knows he cannot harbor them there for the
night, but he drives them to a safe house in the woods, owned by
John Van Trompe, a former Kentucky slaveholder whose conscience compelled him to move to the North and free his slaves. Senator Bird hands John a ten-dollar bill to give to Eliza.

Analysis: Chapters VI–IX

The theme of female virtue dominates this section. Mrs. Shelby and
Mrs. Bird assert their beliefs over and against their husbands'
socially conditioned viewpoints, and, although they lack the more
worldly power of men, they can exert influence within the family
and the household. This figure of the pious, loving mother recurs
throughout the book. Stowe suggests that Eliza's amazing leap onto
the river ice is made possible only through the unique power of a
mother's love, and Eliza earns Mrs. Bird's sympathy in part by
appealing to her grief for her own dead child. Insofar as Stowe
intends many of her female figures, such as Mrs. Shelby and now
Mrs. Bird, to serve a political purpose, these women never develop
into full characters. Rather, they act as models of morality, advocating abolition on a theoretical level, and trying to help the slaves as
much as possible on a practical one.

It is important to note that Stowe's women figures do not assert
their beliefs out of a sense of female independence or defiance per se.
Rather, these women act on religious convictions. Here and
throughout the novel, the value of Christian religious doctrine
emerges as a central theme, serving as the standard of virtue by
which slavery must be deemed wrong. Thus Mrs. Bird cites the Bible

when declaring the injustice of the Fugitive Slave Law of 1850. Still, despite Stowe's use of her female characters to emphasize Christian morality, many readers consider Stowe's women to be proto-feminist figures because they insist upon the significance and value of their own opinions and defy the male characters in doing so.

Eliza's escape across the river is the novel's most famous scene. More than a memorable image from the book, the "miraculous" leap is an important symbol, representing the passage from slavery to freedom and the courage and intrepidity required to make such a passage. However, it is important to realize, as Stowe's readers would have understood, that Eliza's passage into Ohio does not guarantee her freedom. The Fugitive Slave Act barred Northerners from assisting runaway slaves and allowed escaped slaves caught in the North to be returned to their masters in the South. Thus, throughout the novel, anyone who helps Eliza, like the Birds, does so in violation of the law. Eliza must travel all the way to Canada to secure her freedom definitively.

Chapters X–XIII

Summary: Chapter X

Haley has returned to the Shelbys' home to collect Uncle Tom. Aunt Chloe cooks her husband one last meal before he leaves and laments the evils of slavery. He asks her to trust in God to protect them, and tells her that their master is good. Haley takes Tom away, putting his feet in fetters. Mas'r George, who was visiting a friend the previous day, runs up to the wagon in dismay. Haley goes into the blacksmith's to fix Tom's handcuffs, and Tom and Mas'r George converse. George tells Tom that, when he grows older, he will come and save him. For now, he gives Tom a dollar to wear around his neck.

Summary: Chapter XI

In a small country hotel in Kentucky, a sign announces a hunt for a slave named George, who has run away from his master. In the bar room, some men discuss a recently posted sign. The sign reads, "Very light mulatto . . . will probably try to pass for a white man . . . has been branded in his right hand with the letter H . . . I will give four hundred dollars for him alive, and the same sum for satisfactory proof that he has been killed." Mr. Wilson, the owner of a bagging factory, is in the inn and says that this same George once worked for him. Just then, a tall man with Spanish coloring arrives at the inn. He calls himself Henry Butler and is accompanied by a slave named Jim. He looks at the sign and dismisses it, saying he seems to recall meeting a man of that description near a farm they passed along the way. Mr. Wilson looks at the "Spanish man" and realizes that he is George Harris. George invites Mr. Wilson up to his room and tells him that he is now a free man and is escaping to a place that will recognize his freedom. Mr. Wilson, well-meaning but rather unenlightened, tells George he is sorry to see him "breaking the laws of [his] country." George protests that the United States is not "his" country, for slaves neither make nor consent to American laws and gain no protection by them. He asks Mr. Wilson to bring a pin to his wife, whom George believes is still a slave; he also asks Wilson to tell her that he is going to Canada and that she should join him if she can.

Summary: Chapter XII
Meanwhile, Haley and Tom continue toward the slave market. When they stop for the night, Tom must stay in a jail. This insults his dignity as a man who has always been honest and upright. At eleven o'clock the next day, the selling begins, and Haley buys several more slaves. He then boards them all on a ship headed for the Deep South, where they will be sold for plantation work. On the ship, a slave woman jumps overboard after her son is taken from her. Tom hears the splash.

Summary: Chapter XIII
Eliza and Harry arrive at a Quaker settlement, where they stay with a woman named Rachel Halliday. After learning that Eliza's last name is Harris, the Quakers realize that she is the wife of George Harris, who is on his way to the settlement. That night, amid tears, the couple reunites. The next morning, the Quakers and former slaves eat breakfast together, and George and Eliza learn they will have to wait until evening to escape.

Analysis: Chapters X–XIII
Since the publication of *Uncle Tom's Cabin*, the term "Uncle Tom" has entered into the English language as a generic phrase denoting a black person eager to win the approval of whites. This section of the novel gives us our first insight into the term's aptness. Especially in contrast to George, Uncle Tom proves a docile and submissive character. He serves his white owners dutifully, never making any attempt to escape, and praises his master's goodness even as he is

forced to part from his wife as a result of Shelby's actions. In the figure of Tom, we see evidence of Stowe's "romantic racialism." Romantic racialism describes an attitude whereby a person regards another race with a paternalistic kindness—a sense of sympathy tainted by condescension. For while Stowe argues for the fair and humane treatment of African Americans, she also frequently idealizes and romanticizes them, portraying them as quaint or charmingly good-hearted rather than as complex, full human beings.

Yet while we may criticize Stowe's idealized black characters, it is important to note that most of her characters, both white and black, receive rather sentimental treatment. Like Upton Sinclair's *The Jungle*, *Uncle Tom's Cabin* does not aim to present a realistic vision of the world, but rather to argue for a different one—to persuade a particular audience to adopt a particular political position. In the case of *Uncle Tom's Cabin*, Stowe sets out to convince her Northern audience of the evil of slavery; she uses the figure of Uncle Tom not to explore the psychology of a slave, but to assist her thematic arguments. Although Uncle Tom's sense of duty and self-sacrifice have, at times, made Stowe's book an object of ridicule, it was precisely these qualities of magnanimity and gentle patience that made Tom an admirable and moving figure to Stowe's white Northern audience in 1852.

Moreover, Uncle Tom's passivity enables the novel's most trenchant exploration of the conflict between Christian ideals and the cruel inhumanities of slavery. Tom's policy of "turning the other cheek" stems from a religious faith, and thus his behavior may be interpreted as owing less to weakness than to principle. Tom believes in a world beyond this one, and he keeps the notion of his afterlife foremost in his mind, trusting that today's suffering will be tomorrow's salvation. This attitude contrasts strongly with George's lack of faith, evident in his argument with Eliza in Chapter III. By juxtaposing George against Tom in this way, Stowe establishes George as a romantic hero—one who involves himself in a determined struggle to defend his passions—while making Tom a martyr, willing to sacrifice his own interests for the good of the greater cause.

In Chapter XIII, the Quakers appear as a happy medium between these two extremes. While they believe in love and goodwill toward all people, they do not flinch from some amount of civil disobedience in order to help escaping slaves. Throughout the book, Stowe depicts her Quaker characters as people who, in their fight against slavery, always find a way to balance their love for God with their love for humanity.

CHAPTERS XIV–XVI

SUMMARY: CHAPTER XIV

Tom and the other slaves continue to travel down the Mississippi River, joined by travelers and workers headed for New Orleans. Tom has won Haley's confidence with his meek obedience. Therefore, he has received permission to roam the boat freely. He sits up in a nook in the cotton bales, reading his Bible. While there, Tom meets a little girl named Eva St. Clare. An angel of a girl, she dances among the passengers, spreading smiles and good cheer. Tom and Eva quickly become friends, and she tells him she will ask her father, Augustine St. Clare, if he will buy Tom.

One day, Eva falls over the side of the boat, and, while everyone else stands by in shock, Tom plunges over the side of the boat and saves her. Grateful to Tom for rescuing his daughter, St. Clare offers to buy Tom from Haley; Eva urges him to pay whatever price is asked. When her father inquires why she is so intent on buying Tom, she answers that she wants to make Tom happy. St. Clare signs the bill of sale and tells Tom that he shall be in charge of driving the family's coach.

SUMMARY: CHAPTER XV

Here we learn the background of the St. Clare family, beginning with Augustine St. Clare. St. Clare was born to a wealthy planter in Louisiana. Raised by a mother of unparalleled goodness, he grew up soft and gentle. When he became a man, he fell in love with a beautiful woman in the North whom he wanted to marry. However, he received a letter from her guardian saying that she was to marry someone else, and he married a different woman, Marie. After his marriage to Marie, he received a letter from his true love explaining that he had been the victim of deceit, and that she had always loved him. He wrote her back, saying that there was nothing he could do; he was married to Marie, and his heart was broken.

We also learn something about St. Clare's wife. Possessive, materialistic, and vain, Marie irritates everyone around her. She suffers from hundreds of imagined illnesses and constantly complains.

Next the reader learns that, to help him take care of his child and his difficult wife, St. Clare has brought his cousin, Miss Ophelia, to live with him. A robust woman from New England, Ophelia proves industrious and responsible. Although she and St. Clare possess nearly opposite dispositions—St. Clare is passionate and volatile—

they love each other dearly. She regards her years in his New Orleans household as a kind of "project"—a burden that she willingly undertakes for the good of the family.

St. Clare, Eva, and Tom arrive at the house. Adolph, the black doorman, shows Tom into the kitchen, and Marie and St. Clare begin to fight. She berates him for having left her alone too long. He gives her a gift, but she refuses to be placated.

SUMMARY: CHAPTER XVI

The next morning, Marie complains about the slaves, calling them selfish creatures. Eva points out that her mother could not survive without Mammy, an old black woman who sits up long nights with Marie. But Marie grumbles that Mammy talks and thinks too much about her husband and children, from whom Marie has separated her. When St. Clare and Eva exit the room, Marie begins to complain to Miss Ophelia, who generally greets her remarks with blank silence.

In contrast to her mother, Eva remains filled with joy and does all she can to make Tom happy. Ever adoring and generous, she tells Marie that a house full of slaves makes for a much more pleasant life than a house without them because, with slaves, one has more people to love. Extending her affection lavishly on everyone, Eva gives no thought to the differences between blacks and whites.

ANALYSIS: CHAPTERS XIV–XVI

Stowe's idealization of Little Eva is matched only by her idealization of Uncle Tom. Both characters manifest supreme virtue and goodness, furthering the book's religious messages. Because of Eva's status as an innocent child, she poses no threat to readers. For this reason, Stowe can use her to voice what was then a radical view of religious thought and racial equality.

While Eva's character is highly idealized, Miss Ophelia receives what may be the most realistic treatment of any female in the book. While Stowe's other women—Mrs. Shelby, Mrs. Bird, and Rachel Halliday, for example—tend to appear as only slightly varying versions of the "perfect" wife-mother, Miss Ophelia approaches the world without the bleeding heart of these characters. Educated and independent, Miss Ophelia is motivated not by feminine emotion, but by rational thought and a sense of practical duty. The reader has seen how Stowe uses her other women characters to prod gently at her readers' consciences, as well as to appeal particularly to Northern mothers and wives who may have had moral influence in their households. With Miss Ophelia, the author may be diversifying her strategy. While Stowe plays on the emotions of deep-feeling mothers, she also aims to speak to women more like St. Clare's independent cousin. An intellectually adept Northern woman, Miss Ophelia is informed about the issues surrounding slavery but has not yet examined her own prejudices. The reader can see evidence of Miss Ophelia's unconscious prejudice in her reaction to Eva's color-blind displays of affection. Eva tries to convince her cousin that they should all be motivated by love, and although Miss Ophelia agrees on a theoretical level, she still recoils at the thought of the girl kissing and hugging the slaves.

Unlike Miss Ophelia, St. Clare is less moved by what he "should" do than by what he feels. This allows him to denounce slavery without hesitation and without considering logical consequences of abolition. Yet this passion without practicality leads to a policy in which St. Clare condemns slavery without taking action to eradicate it. Stowe thus treats St. Clare with much of the same irony she extended to Mr. Shelby. As Stowe develops the main theme of her novel—the evil of slavery and its incompatibility with Christian morality—she continually explores ambiguous characters and situations that seem either to justify or to excuse the practice of slavery. St. Clare and Shelby, good men who own slaves and act as kindly masters to them, provide two of the most interesting of these ambiguous characters. Good men and good masters, they offer a test case for the institution of slavery. Stowe seeks to show that the institution is so inherently evil as to render oxymoronic the notion of "beneficent" slavery or "benign" slaveholders.

Stowe portrays the slave-master relationship as creating an intolerable gulf in power, class, liberty and education, even when it exists between two mutually well-meaning men such as Shelby and Tom, who earnestly care for each other's welfare. This gulf first becomes clear when Shelby smokes his cigar to soothe himself for cleaving Tom's family apart. And now the reader sees the romantic and sentimental St. Clare arguing with Ophelia on behalf of the humanity of his slaves while he continues to own them as property. In the years prior to the Civil War, many people excused slavery by claiming that most slaveholders were good men or acted in the interest of their slaves. Stowe uses her irony to argue against this idea. She implies that the slaves' interests do not lie in having kind masters; instead, they lie in being set free. Any man who owns slaves automatically acts against his slaves' best interests simply by continuing to own them. The role of women in *Uncle Tom's Cabin* undergoes a slight complication in these chapters, as the reader encounters women who do not fit into the religious feminine ideal that Stowe has offered so far. Not only does Ophelia differ from previously presented women; Marie offers a sharp contrast to those ideal types. The grating presence of Marie may serve to emphasize the goodness of the women whom Stowe seeks to uphold as models. Moreover, Marie seems to be intended to represent a white woman who is inferior to her own slaves in her personal qualities. This inferiority of character challenges the assumed white-black moral hierarchy.

Chapters XVII–XIX

Summary: Chapter XVII

Back at the home of the Quakers, Eliza and George speak of the happiness they receive from being in each other's company. They discuss their plans for reaching Canada and realize that a long and dangerous journey awaits them. Phineas, the Quaker who is to drive them to their next stopping-place, tells them that Tom Loker and his gang have arrived at a nearby tavern and plan to come for them that very night. After supper, Phineas, George, Eliza, Harry, and the Hallidays leave the house, hoping to elude their pursuers under cover of darkness. They hurry along, and set up camp in a small space accessible only through a narrow gap between two rocks. If the gang comes to attack them, the men will have to enter one by one.

Tom Loker and his gang arrive, and George stands up on a rock to address them. He asserts his freedom and declares his intention to defend it by force. They shoot at him, but he leaps out the way, swearing that he will shoot any man who tries to enter their campsite. Tom Loker tries to push up and through the rock, and George lives up to his word, wounding him in the side. Loker leaps around until Phineas pushes him over the embankment. The other slave hunters start to fight but eventually retreat, deserting Loker. The Quakers and escaped slaves now approach the slave hunter, wounded and unconscious. Eliza takes pity on Loker, and the Quakers agree to carry him to another Quaker household, where he will be healed. They load the wounded man into their wagon.

SUMMARY: CHAPTER XVIII

"... an't [heaven] where white folks is gwine? I'd rather
go to torment, and get away from Mas'r and Missis."
(See QUOTATIONS, p. 54)

In the St. Clare household, Uncle Tom slowly takes on more and more responsibility, eventually taking over the finances of the house for his master. His Christian faith keeps him honest and leads him to worry for St. Clare, who spends his nights at parties in drunken revelry. After a talk with Tom, St. Clare promises to stop this behavior. While Tom attempts to reform his master, Miss Ophelia tries to reform the house. Dinah, the cook, demonstrates a culinary genius but keeps no semblance of order. Miss Ophelia cleans up the kitchen, organizes the house, and attempts to instill a Northern sense of efficiency, with some success.

Prue, a slave from down the street, comes into the kitchen bearing hot rolls to sell. Prue says she is miserable and wishes she were dead. In response to the remark of another slave, she admits to getting drunk in order to alleviate her sorrows. As she leaves the kitchen, Tom asks to help her with carrying the rolls. He implores her to stop drinking and find the Lord. She tells him her sordid history. A former master used her to breed children to sell at the slave market. After being sold to her current master, she gave birth to another baby and gratefully anticipated being able to raise the child, having had so many taken from her over the years. However, her mistress soon took ill, and the long hours that Prue had to spend at her bedside, away from the baby, caused her milk to dry up. Her owners refused to pay for purchased milk, and the baby died of starvation.

After Prue leaves, Tom sits alone outside. Eva comes out to take a ride in her new carriage, and asks him what troubles him. He tells her Prue's story, and she loses all desire to go out that day.

SUMMARY: CHAPTER XIX

A few days later, the members of the St. Clare household learn that Prue's master has whipped her to death. Miss Ophelia reacts with shock, and asks if no laws exist to protect against such deeds. St. Clare explains that the law considers slaves to be property, and people may destroy their own possessions at will. Ophelia accuses St. Clare of supporting slavery; he denies this but says, "in a community so organized, what can a man of honorable and humane feelings do, but shut his eyes all he can, and harden his heart? . . . the most I can do is to try and keep out of the way of it."

Despite this apparent resignation, St. Clare also shows anger against the system and tells of his mother's moral perfection: "a direct embodiment and personification of the New Testament," she possessed a love of humanity that contrasted sharply with his father's aristocratic attitudes, lack of religious sentiment, and embrace of slavery. Although she never confronted his father directly, St. Clare's mother made a great impression upon his moral constitution. Thus when St. Clare and his twin brother inherited the family's slaves upon their father's death, he found himself unable to bear being the master of a huge plantation and hundreds of slaves. St. Clare tells of a slave who was caught trying to run from the plantation. He explains that the slave had a reputation for rebelliousness, but St. Clare, by tending to him and caring for him, "tamed" him. He then made out free papers for the slave. But the slave felt so grateful toward St. Clare that he ripped the papers in two and pledged his life to him. Eva, who is also listening to the story, starts crying and says that hearing these things makes them sink into her heart.

Later, Tom tries to write a letter to his wife and children, but his limited literacy causes him trouble. Eva agrees to help him, and together they write a letter, which Tom sends.

ANALYSIS: CHAPTERS XVII–XIX

The standoff in Chapter XVII between the escaping slaves and Tom Loker's gang provides one of the most dramatically compelling moments in *Uncle Tom's Cabin*, bringing to a crisis the conflict between the escaped slaves' noble dignity and the slave hunters' detestable cruelty. Stowe, who often uses the technique of directly addressing the reader, takes the opportunity to point out that if George were a man in Hungary he would be seen as a hero, but because he is a black man in America he is not. In this way, she attempts to simplify and sentimentalize the situation in such a way that her readers will identify with the heroism of George's stand.

One of Stowe's most effective techniques of persuasion lies in her presentation of the slaves as real human beings. That is, although Stowe does not portray them with a high degree of "realism" per se, she does render them human to her white audience. In 1852, whites lived such separate lives from blacks that Stowe could dislodge some of their prejudices simply by presenting blacks interacting as a family or feeling joy and sorrow. If she could make whites in the North realize that many of the escaping slaves had families, histories, and pressing human reasons to escape the system of slavery, she could make them see the institution in a new light. Historians have argued that Stowe succeeded in this project, effectively breaking through the familiar defenses of the slave system. By forcing her readers to see the institution from a new perspective, not dulled by custom and familiarity, Stowe may have helped to change many people's attitudes.

Stowe's attempts to render the slaves human prove integral to her powerful portrayal of Prue in the next chapter. Having begun to humanize the slaves, she shows a slave who has been dehumanized by the system. If George's attempt to escape explores the theme of slavery from the standpoint of a noble hero, the story of Prue explores the same theme from the standpoint of a tragic victim. Although Stowe has had her characters discuss at length the evils of slavery, she now illustrates her point graphically, intending to shock the reader on a deeply emotional level. Until Stowe introduces Prue, all of the slaves seem to receive comparably decent treatment; the most cruelty they suffer seems to come when they are between owners, in trade and in transit. But slavery ruins Prue, even before it literally claims her life. She has been treated as nothing more than an animal—useful for breeding other animals to sell—and she has been destroyed morally and psychologically. Whether or not Prue's story achieves its desired effect on the reader, it definitively converts Miss Ophelia, who realizes suddenly the institution's wickedness.

Miss Ophelia's outrage at Prue's fate, along with her ensuing discussion with St. Clare, helps to shed light on the man's character. Basically a good-hearted man, he nonetheless feels that he has no choice but to uphold a system of which he disapproves. This contradiction attests to the pernicious power of the slavery, forceful enough to override individual decency. Indeed, many people in 1850s America found slavery fundamentally repugnant, and yet the system persisted. The conversation between Miss Ophelia and St. Clare explores how this is possible. In St. Clare's description of his father, he explains how much depends on the moral lines that an individual chooses to draw. While one may stand for freedom, one can choose to apply the ideal to men only, to whites only, or to white male landowners only.

Eva's assistance to Tom in writing his letter serves as a small ray of hope in Chapter XIX. Stowe makes an innocent child her instrument for hope as she demonstrates how an act of nonjudgmental love can help the oppressed to find their own voices, to write their own words, and attest to their own humanity.

Chapters XX–XXIII

Summary: Chapter XX

St. Clare buys a young slave named Topsy, who has never received any education, and gives her to Miss Ophelia to tutor. Miss Ophelia protests, but St. Clare tells her that Topsy's previous owners have abused her. He notes that the child's back bears multiple scars. He also points out that, in teaching Topsy, Ophelia would be fulfilling a role akin to that of a missionary. This statement awakens Ophelia's conscience and she agrees to take on Topsy's instruction. However, Topsy proves disobedient and wild, unacquainted with the conventions of Christian behavior. After she steals a pair of gloves, Ophelia presses her to confess her other sins, and she confesses falsely to stealing other items. Later, Topsy explains that she had nothing to confess but wanted to oblige the older woman. When Eva speaks a few words of kindness to the girl, Topsy looks at her in bewilderment, having never heard kindness before. Still, the young slave and Eva quickly become friends, and traipse about playing together. But Topsy remains just as unmanageable as before. Ophelia tries to teach Topsy the catechism, but the girl fails to understand even its words, and thus she recites them back mangled and confused, without any comprehension of their meaning.

Summary: Chapter XXI

Back on the farm in Kentucky, Aunt Chloe receives Tom's letter. Though Mr. Shelby's business remains fraught with debt, Mrs. Shelby wants to try to raise enough money to buy Tom back. Mr. Shelby begins to shout and tells her not to meddle in his affairs. Chloe calls Mrs. Shelby outside, ostensibly to look at the chickens, and asks to be hired out to make cakes and pies to help earn money for Tom. Mrs. Shelby agrees.

Summary: Chapter XXII

Two years pass while Tom serves the St. Clares. He gets a letter from Mas'r George telling about life in Kentucky and about the studies he has undertaken. Tom and Eva grow increasingly close; he gives her little gifts, and she reads the Bible aloud to him.

The whole family goes out to a villa on Lake Pontchartrain for the summer, hoping to escape the heat of the city. Tom and Eva sit together in the villa's garden, reading the Prophecies and the Revelation, and Tom sings hymns about the new Jerusalem and angels.

Eva says that she has seen angels, and points up to the sky. She declares that she will be joining them in heaven soon. Miss Ophelia calls them inside and reminds them that Eva has been sick and should not spend too long outdoors. Ophelia worries about the child's cough, and Tom notices that she has grown thinner.

SUMMARY: CHAPTER XXIII

St. Clare's brother Alfred visits with his son, Henrique. Eva and Henrique enjoy playing together, but, one day, Henrique strikes his slave, Dodo, because he has allowed Henrique's horse to get dusty. Eva reacts with sadness, asking Henrique how he could act so wickedly. He responds with incomprehension, and, after Dodo saddles the horse, he gives the slave money so that he may go buy candy for himself. Eva thanks Dodo for his work, and Dodo appreciates Eva's gesture far more than Henrique's. The fathers watch what has happened and begin to argue about slavery. St. Clare says that soon the slaves will rise up; Alfred replies that he will keep them down as long as possible. Eva and Henrique return, and she asks him to love Dodo. He says that he will, because he would do anything that she asked.

ANALYSIS: CHAPTERS XX–XXIII

This section emphasizes the importance of love—both Christian and romantic—in eradicating slavery and its mindset. The reader notes the value of Christian love through its absence, as Miss Ophelia teaches Topsy the catechism without conveying the spirit of it. Because Ophelia forces Topsy to memorize the words without any sense of the emotions behind them, it is no surprise when Topsy spews the prayer back in a mangled and confused form. Without love, the words are simply meaningless sounds. As we have seen, Stowe uses Ophelia as a kind of surrogate within the book for her Northern audience. Now she suggests to these readers that for them, as for Ophelia, it is not enough to support abolition out of a sense of duty alone. Their anti-slavery sentiments must stem from a deeper place, from a love for human beings.

Romantic love also comes to play a role in fighting slavery as both Aunt Chloe and Mrs. Shelby demonstrate through their paralleled devotion to their respective husbands. Chloe resolves to work to help buy Tom out of slavery, while Mrs. Shelby endeavors to help her husband with his money matters. Both women try to free their husbands with their love—to free Uncle Tom on a literal level, and to free Mr. Shelby from his financial straights. In portraying the redemptive power of love as embodied in these two women, Stowe mixes love and her feminist theme, once again giving power to her female characters and depicting them as wiser than their male counterparts. Moreover, Stowe's feminism here may extend beyond a mere indication of the insight and virtue of women to a directly political observation. As the reader sees in this section, although Mrs. Shelby enjoys much freedom relative to her slave, she remains in a similarly subjected state. Like Mrs. Bird in Chapter IX, she must appear to stand behind her husband and pursue her own causes through him, even if she does not support his opinions and actions. Stowe seems to suggest the folly in such a convention.

Yet while Stowe may hint at the oppression of women, she focuses primarily on the oppression of blacks, and the argument between St. Clare and Alfred in Chapter XXIII contains one of the most honest discussions of slavery in the book. Alfred openly admits his desire to keep slaves, as well as their own desire not to be slaves. Logical and upfront about the issue, he does not try to make excuses for himself. Both brothers seem to regard the enslavement of others as a natural human tendency. Stowe suggests that people possess an innate greed and an innate love of power and that the system of slavery results directly from these human failings. Accordingly, Stowe implies that, to abolish slavery, people should not resort to complicated political maneuverings; instead, they must learn to curb innate human impulses on a fundamental level. And in this section she strongly intimates that the agent of that change will be love—the kind of love Eva exhibits toward Dodo in this chapter.

A simple but important instance of foreshadowing occurs in Chapter XXII, when Eva and Tom read the Bible, and Eva says that she will soon be going to heaven to join the angels. Tom notices that Eva does not look well, but the text does not explore the matter further. Stowe uses this scene to foreshadow Eva's eventual death in Chapter XXVI. The young girl's apparent foreknowledge of her own death introduces a perhaps unfortunate piece of nineteenth-century melodrama, but it does serve to underscore Eva's basic saintliness and goodness. The little girl is so pure that she is already in touch with heaven. The fact of Eva's moral perfection adds authority to her loving actions and puts extra force behind her innocent but political observations.

CHAPTERS XXIV–XXVIII

SUMMARY: CHAPTER XXIV

Alfred and Henrique end their visit. Eva's health begins to fail. Marie, who has never shown any interest in her child before, now begins to moan in motherly despair, saying that her child is dying, and that the impending tragedy affects her more than anyone else. At one point, Eva appears to recover, but the episode proves only a deceptive lull in her decline. However, she continues to treat the slaves generously, telling Tom that she would die for the slaves of the South if it would alleviate their suffering. She talks to her father and asks him if all the slaves could be set free; she asks him to work for their freedom as she would have if she had lived beyond childhood. He says that he will do what he can but does promise to free Tom if she dies. She tells him she will soon go to the savior's house and pleads with him to follow her there one day.

SUMMARY: CHAPTER XXV

On a Sunday afternoon, Marie lounges on the veranda complaining to St. Clare when Miss Ophelia comes in indignantly, saying that she can no longer stand Topsy. St. Clare asks her how, if her Gospel cannot suffice to save one child, she expects missionaries to go out among thousands. Eva, who has been sitting on her father's lap, now hops down and beckons silently to Topsy to follow her. They enter a little glass room at the corner of the veranda. She asks Topsy if she loves anyone. Topsy replies that she has been deprived of all family, left alone in the world without anyone to love or to love her in return. Eva tells her that Miss Ophelia would love her if she were good. Topsy laughs and says that Miss Ophelia cannot even bear to have Topsy touch her, because Topsy is black. Eva lays her hand on Topsy's shoulder and tells her that she loves her, and tells her that she should be good for her sake. She adds that Jesus loves her as well. Topsy begins to cry and promises to try to be good.

The adults have overheard the conversation, and Miss Ophelia tells St. Clare that she always has had a prejudice against blacks, and that it is true that she could never bear to have Topsy touch her. She had not realized, however, that Topsy had known this. She says she wishes she could learn to shed some of her prejudices, and suggests that Eva might teach her.

Summary: Chapter XXVI

Eva requests that Miss Ophelia cut some of the curls from her hair; she then asks that all the slaves be convened. Lying weakly in her bed, she addresses the slaves, telling them to be good Christians and love one another. Then she gives each of them a lock of her hair by which to remember her. Later, after the slaves have left the room, Eva asks her father if he is a Christian and tells him of the land she soon will enter. He sees the fervor in her heart but fails to feel it himself. At last, Eva dies as St. Clare, Ophelia, and Marie look on. St. Clare asks her to tell them what she sees, and she replies, "Oh! love,—joy,—peace!"

Summary: Chapter XXVII

After Eva's funeral, the house enters into mourning, but the slaves are unable to express their grief, because Marie demands all of their attention. Marie screams and carries on, but St. Clare is too deep in mourning to shed a single tear. Tom talks to St. Clare of the glory of heaven, but St. Clare finds himself incapable of believing. He longs to find God, but he feels that when he prays, no one is listening. Uncle Tom prays for him when his master cannot. When St. Clare hears Tom pray, he almost feels the awakening of faith inside himself.

Summary: Chapter XXVIII

Ophelia reports to her brother that she has managed to reform Topsy's wild ways. She asks St. Clare to give her legal ownership of Topsy, in order that she might take her to the North and set her free. She has instilled in Topsy the values of Christianity but knows that the experiences of slavery would beat them back out of her. St. Clare writes the deed then and there, at his sister's insistence. Ophelia then asks if he has made provision for his other slaves. She reminds him that, in the case of his death, they might go to cruel owners. St. Clare says he will provide for them someday. He then goes off to a café to read the newspaper and is stabbed in a fight between two drunken men. Other men from the café take St. Clare home, who is laid out on a shutter. St. Clare asks Tom to pray for him and then mumbles his own prayers. He says he is coming home at last. Just before he dies, his eyes open and he says with joy, "Mother!"

Analysis: Chapters XXIX–XXXIII

Critics of *Uncle Tom's Cabin* often find fault with the novel's excessive sentimentality and melodrama. These chapters, dealing with the deaths of Eva and St. Clare, figure among the most sentimental

in the book; over the scene of Eva's death in particular, Stowe
intones with overbearing force:

> Farewell, beloved child! the bright, eternal doors have closed
> after thee; we shall see thy sweet face no more. Oh, woe for
> them who watched thy entrance into heaven, when they shall
> wake and find only the cold gray sky of daily life, and thou
> gone forever!

Stowe emphasizes repeatedly Eva's perfection, her exemplary Christianity, her true innocence, her angelic nature. However, Stowe renders Eva in this way not merely for the sake of indulging in the thrill
of histrionic grief, or to infuse her book with spectacle. Rather,
Stowe idealizes Eva in order to raise issues of religion via the vision
of heaven and the immortal soul. Indeed, Eva appears as a Christ figure as she lies dying—a perfect being without sin, she allows others
to find salvation through her death. In asking Ophelia to clip her
curls, Eva asks to be "sheared," thus again referencing Jesus Christ.
Ophelia even says outright that she hopes to be more like Eva,
because Eva is like Christ. The use of Christ figures becomes a minor
motif in *Uncle Tom's Cabin*, underscoring some of the book's religious themes. The motif will appear again during the scene of Uncle
Tom's tragic death in Chapter XLI.

After Eva's death, Stowe briefly explores the conflict surrounding
St. Clare's religious skepticism, as his persistent inability to find God
clashes with Tom's earnest desire to see his master find salvation.
And this brief conflict paves the way for another climatic moment of
intense sentimentality, this one as overtly religious as the last. As St.
Clare lies dying, he finally discovers a religious sign, as he appar-
ently sees his mother, an idealized being like Eva. In this way, Stowe
emphasizes the moral power of Christianity to transform and save
the soul—a power that Stowe hoped would eventually alter the
hearts of the slaveholders and lead to the eradication of slavery.

This section witnesses not only St. Clare's conversion, but Miss
Ophelia's as well. Ophelia finally acknowledges her prejudices, realizing the truth of Eva's words. She knows that she must love Topsy
as a Christian in order to help her. St. Clare's comments also contribute to the conversion. When he asks Miss Ophelia what good her
faith is if she cannot save one child, she realizes that the love mod-
eled by Eva constitutes the next step in her work with Topsy.

Chapters XXIX–XXXIII

Summary: Chapter XXIX

Though St. Clare promised Eva that he would make arrangements for the slaves and that he would free Tom after she died, his own death came so suddenly that he had no time to act on his promise. Thus all of the St. Clare slaves find themselves the property of Marie. The cruel woman sends Rosa out to a whipping, previously unheard of at the St. Clare house, and then agrees to sell all of the slaves. Miss Ophelia pleads on their behalf, but Marie says that it would be worse for the slaves to be set free than to be kept in the system of slavery. She sends them off to the slave warehouse.

Summary: Chapter XXX

The narrator introduces two slave women in the warehouse, Susan and Emmeline, a mother and her beautiful daughter of fifteen. Emmeline has wondrously curly hair, but her mother combs it all out flat, in the hope that she will look less attractive and not be noticed by men who are buying female slaves for their pleasure. Before the women are brought to the selling-block, however, the seller tells Emmeline to go curl her hair—such an enhancement could bring in an extra hundred dollars. Uncle Tom now comes up for sale also. Simon Legree, a crude and evil-looking man who owns a cotton plantation, buys both Uncle Tom and Emmeline, as well as two other men.

Summary: Chapter XXXI

Legree chains Tom's hands and feet and puts the slaves on a boat headed for his plantation. Legree takes all that Tom owns, except for his Bible, which Tom has hidden in his pocket. Legree does find his hymnbook, however, and tells him that his plantation tolerates no religion. He then shakes his fist in the slaves' faces, declaring it hard as iron and well-suited for "knocking down niggers."

Summary: Chapter XXXII

As they travel, Legree leers at Emmeline, promising that she will have "fine times" with him. Legree lives all alone on the plantation, with only slaves to keep him company. He keeps two black overseers, whom he treats with some familiarity, yet he attempts to make them brutal toward the under-slaves. He also has one slave woman, Cassy, living with him in his quarters. He has bought Emmeline to replace her. The plantation proves a horrific place, where even the slaves treat each other cruelly. Tom's religious belief falters, but then he sees a vision of Eva, which renews his faith and his strength. He works diligently and tries to help the other slaves.

SUMMARY: CHAPTER XXXIII
One day, as Tom works in the cotton fields, Cassy comes and works alongside the other slaves. Tom sees another slave woman struggling to fill her sack, and so Tom helps her, and then Cassy helps him. The overseers see the slaves cooperating and report back to Legree. When Tom and the women bring in their baskets, Legree tells Tom to whip the woman. He refuses, and the two overseers drag him outside, where they beat him nearly to death.

ANALYSIS: CHAPTERS XXIX–XXXIII
Stowe has spent much of the novel exploring morally ambiguous forms of slavery in order to expose their underlying evil. She has noted the insidious wickedness inherent in even the "benevolent" slavery practiced by otherwise decent men such as Shelby and St. Clare. Now, however, Stowe at last tears the mask of gentility off the slave system and shows what can happen when slaves live with cruel masters. Stowe uses the conversation between Emmeline and her mother to appeal specifically to women with children. Under the slave system, young girls could be purchased to act essentially as prostitutes, and Legree purchases Emmeline with this purpose in mind. In the previous sections, Stowe has approached the theme of slavery with the persuasive niceties of debate. However, in this section, she offers a visceral, emotional appeal against slavery based on the power of shock and moral outrage. If the goodness of Tom has not won the reader over to her position, she hopes that the evil of Legree will have a stronger effect.

In her presentation of Tom's trials after St. Clare's death, Stowe makes a point about slavery at large, a point she repeats throughout the book. Namely, a slave's fate lies at the mercy of his master, and a master's legal claim on a slave overrides all efforts by others to improve the slave's welfare. Thus Miss Ophelia can do nothing to stop Marie. Marie can whip the slaves or sell them into further cycles of abuse. Stowe emphasizes the importance of religion and love and their ability to transform the heart, but in this section she does not shy away from the horrific evil that exists in their absence.

Stowe focuses not only on the effect of slavery on slaves but also on its effect on the slaves' owners. While slavery causes emotional and physical suffering among the slaves that slaveholders can never know, the system also makes human beings lose all sense of right and wrong. This latter effect extends to both the oppressed and the oppressor. Through the story of the Legree plantation, Stowe shows how the system turns slaves against each other—how cruelty makes people crueler. The plantation also lacks all sense of religion. Tom tries to fight against the cruelty, to infuse goodness into this moral void. The only commands he refuses to obey are those that go against his faith; thus in the scene of the beating in Chapter XXXIII, he holds strong. These pages work toward transforming Tom into a martyr-figure. He would rather face a severe beating himself than violate his principles by beating another slave.

CHAPTERS XXXIV–XXXVIII

SUMMARY: CHAPTER XXXIV
Cassy comes to Tom and tries to heal him after his flogging, giving him water and cleaning his wounds. She tells him that no hope exists for the slaves and that he should just give up. She explains that there is no God. Tom urges her not to let the wicked acts of others make her wicked herself. He argues that to become evil would constitute the worst punishment possible. Cassy starts to moan and then tells her story.

Cassy is a mulatto, a woman who is one-half black. She grew up in luxury, the daughter of a rich white man, and became the mistress of a lawyer. She had several children and was happy, but then the lawyer fell in love with another woman and sold her and her children to a new master. That master sold her children and then sold her to a third man, by whom she had a child. When the baby was a few weeks old, she poisoned it in order to prevent herself the pain of having her children taken from her again. She continued to be passed from man to man until she came to Legree.

SUMMARY: CHAPTER XXXV
Legree feels emotional attachment to Cassy, even though she scorns Legree and his ways. As they argue one day, Sambo, one of the overseers, comes into the house with the lock of Eva's hair that Tom had tied around his neck. It twines around Legree's finger as if it were alive, and he screams, throwing it off into the fire.

We now learn Legree's history. Legree grew up with a kind and loving mother but a brutal father. He took after his father and ignored his mother's advice. His mother nonetheless clung to him, loving him, but he broke away at an early age and sought a life at sea. He later received a letter with a curl of her hair enclosed. His mother wrote that she was dying, but that she blessed and forgave him. The text explains that the lock of Eva's hair reminded him of this tragic occurrence. He has turned to drink in order to forget his mother, but the image of the hair still haunts him.

Angry, he leaves the house to go to find Emmeline. He can only hear a hymn being sung by the slaves, and thinks he sees some sort of ghost in the fog. He feels a deep fear of Tom's spiritual power.

SUMMARY: CHAPTER XXXVI
The next day, Cassy tells Legree to leave Tom alone from now on. Forgetting his fear of the previous night, he ignores her advice and goes to talk to Tom, to tell him to get down on his knees and beg Legree's pardon. Tom refuses. Legree threatens him, but Tom says that he has a vision of eternity to look forward to, and Legree can do nothing to harm him.

SUMMARY: CHAPTER XXXVII
George and Eliza have successfully arrived at the next Quaker settlement and leave Tom Loker with the first group of Quakers to be nursed back to health. After he recovers, Tom abandons his evil ways and lives with the Quakers as a changed man, in great admiration of their life. George and Eliza continue on, disguising themselves and eventually reaching freedom in Canada.

SUMMARY: CHAPTER XXXVIII
Back on the plantation, Uncle Tom once again feels his faith falter. Legree taunts him and leaves him to his doubts. But then Tom sings a hymn and sees Jesus Christ, who comes and speaks to him. His strength is once again renewed, and he sings songs of joy. Even when Legree beats him, he feels filled with the Lord's spirit.

Cassy comes to him in the night and tells him that she wants to kill Legree. Tom tells her not to, because it is a sin. He pleads with her to try to escape instead. She says that she will, and that she will try to do so without bloodshed.

ANALYSIS: CHAPTERS XXXIV–XXXVIII
In previous chapters, the text has explored the effect of religion on slavery—how Christian values and Christian love can expose the inherent evil of treating a human being as property. Now, however,

in the scenes depicting the Legree plantation, the text turns to examine the effect of slavery on religion. While earlier chapters have noted the ways in which slavery may cause moral devastation, these chapters attempt to illustrate the threat of slavery, not only to a person's belief in Christian morality but to the God behind that morality. The text illustrates this notion through Tom, who struggles to maintain his faith. Indeed, the central conflict of this section of the book takes place within Tom as he endeavors to cling to his beliefs despite the wickedness and suffering that impinges on him.

Tom feels strengthened in his struggle by his vision of Jesus in the fire. The text parallels this vision with the vision seen by Legree, of the ghost in the fog. The motif of supernaturalism effectively serves to emphasize the moral contrast between the wicked slaveholder and the virtuous slave. While Tom's vision comes as a reward to him for his goodness, soothing and encouraging him, Legree's vision comes as a punishment, terrifying and warning him. Together, the visions allude to a higher order, evaluating the behavior of mortals and visiting apparitions upon them accordingly. The text thus implies that the basic structure of the universe essentially opposes the evil of slavery, bolstering its victims and seeking revenge on its perpetrators. In some sense, this idea of a fundamentally moral universe plagued with human corruption can explain the few other "supernatural" occurrences in *Uncle Tom's Cabin*, such as Eliza's leap over the river and Eva's foreknowledge of her own death.

This section also explores morality from the female perspective. Legree's mother serves as another example of the good mother figure that arises again and again throughout the book. Cassy, in contrast, serves as an example of a good mother turned bad. Under slavery, the very power of maternal love can become violent, and its fierce sense of protection can be perverted to the point that a mother can kill her own child. The compelling contrast illustrates slavery's destructive influence on morality.

The contrast between these two mother figures joins a number of similarly pointed parallels and contrasts throughout the text of *Uncle Tom's Cabin*. The text repeatedly employs such couplings as a rhetorical tool, showing the superiority of one side of the pair over the other. Thus, it establishes oppositions between slavery and Christian love, or between an idealized girl such as Eva and a vicious woman such as Marie. The novel also uses parallelism and counterpart as a structural device, dividing itself into two main plots, the story of Uncle Tom and the story of George and Eliza. The "slave narrative" of Uncle Tom contrasts with the "escape narrative" of George and Eliza. As George and Eliza grow closer to freedom, Tom finds himself in more oppressive conditions of slavery. The interrelationship between the two serves to highlight the triumphs of George and Eliza and the sorrows of Uncle Tom, endowing both stories with extra force.

As George and Eliza reach Canada and freedom, Tom finds oppression and death in rural Louisiana. In this contrast, the reader begins to see the symbolic function of geography in the novel. As the two plots diverge, one moving to the North and the other to the South, the North becomes synonymous with freedom, and the South with slavery. Obviously, these symbols have roots in historical reality. But it is important to note how Stowe works this geographical contrast into her structural technique, creating increasingly disparate settings in which to portray the increasingly disparate conditions of the novel's main characters.

CHAPTERS XXXIX–XLV

SUMMARY: CHAPTER XXXIX

Cassy devises a plan to make Legree think that ghosts haunt the garret of the house. Then she and Emmeline conspicuously attempt an escape, running from the house and into the nearby swamp. The overseers order a hunt, and while the household searches for the women, they slip back into the house and into the garret, where Cassy has been hoarding food and supplies. Cassy and Emmeline can remain safely in the garret, for Legree and the others will attribute any noises they make to the "ghosts" and will never dare to venture upstairs to investigate.

SUMMARY: CHAPTER XL

> "Oh, Mas'r! . . . Do the worst you can, my troubles'll be over soon; but, if ye don't repent, yours won't never end!"
>
> (See QUOTATIONS, p. 55)

Unable to act on his fury over Cassy and Emmeline's escape, Legree directs his wrath toward Tom. He suspects that Tom knows something about the women's plan and sends for him for questioning.

He tells Tom that he will kill him if Tom does not tell him what he knows about the women's escape, but Tom says that he would rather die than speak. Legree pauses for a moment, as if good and evil were battling inside his heart, but evil wins. Legree beats Tom all night, and then he orders Sambo and Quimbo, the overseers, to continue the beating. Tom prays and remains pious to the end, touching Sambo and Quimbo's hearts. They believe him when he tells them of Jesus. Tom prays that their hearts can be saved.

SUMMARY: CHAPTER XLI

> *"Witness, eternal God! . . . [F]rom this hour, I will do what one man can to drive out this curse of slavery from my land!"*
>
> (*See* QUOTATIONS, *p. 56*)

Two days later, George Shelby, Mr. Shelby's son, arrives at Legree's plantation. He has spent much time searching for his beloved former slave after the death of his father. George finds Tom near death, but Tom is delighted to see "Mas'r George" after their long separation, and he dies a contented man. George takes Tom's body and tells Legree that he will have him tried for murder. Legree points out that no whites witnessed the flogging, and thus the case could not go to court. George strikes him and knocks him to the ground. The other slaves plead with him to buy them, but he cannot. As he leaves, he resolves to do all he can to abolish slavery.

SUMMARY: CHAPTER XLII

Cassy, disguised as a Creole Spanish lady, escapes from the plantation with Emmeline. They board the same boat as George Shelby, who notices Cassy. Fearing that he sees through her disguise, she tells him everything. George promises to protect her to the best of his abilities. The passenger in the next cabin, a French woman named Madame de Thoux, asks George questions about his home and realizes that George Harris, Eliza's husband, is her brother. Madame de Thoux was born into slavery like her brother, but she was later sold to a kind man who took her to the West Indies, set her free, and married her. Her husband died only recently. Cassy, too, has listened to George Shelby's story, and when she hears his description of Eliza, she realizes that Eliza may be her daughter.

SUMMARY: CHAPTER XLIII

Cassy, Emmeline, and Madame de Thoux travel to Montreal, where George and Eliza Harris are living. George works in a machinist's shop, and Eliza has given birth to a second child, a daughter. The five reunite with tears and joy. Madame de Thoux's husband has recently died and left her a great fortune, which she offers to the family. From Canada, they sail to France, where they live for a few years before returning to the United States. In a letter to one of his friends, George advocates the immigration of blacks to Liberia, a West African nation founded by private organizations and the U. S. government in order to resettle freed slaves. George and his family immigrate to Liberia and are not heard from again.

SUMMARY: CHAPTER XLIV

> "...Think of your freedom, every time you see UNCLE
> TOM'S CABIN; and let it be a memorial to put you all
> in mind to follow in his steps...."
> (See QUOTATIONS, p. 57)

When George Shelby returns home he tells Chloe about Tom. He then gives free papers to all of the slaves. They ask him not to send them away, but he tells them that he will pay them wages, and that when he dies they will be free. He relates to them the story of Uncle Tom's death and asks them to think of their freedom each time they see Tom's cabin.

SUMMARY: CHAPTER XLV

Chapter XLV serves more as an epilogue than a chapter proper. Here Stowe offers an author's note, or set of "concluding remarks," in which she declares that most of the events of the story actually occurred, not among the characters mentioned, but in the lives of various people at various times. She makes a direct and impassioned appeal to Northerners and Southerners alike to end slavery in the name of Christianity, and of God.

ANALYSIS: CHAPTERS XXXIX–XLV

In this final section, Uncle Tom's martyrdom shines forth, and in his death he evokes Christ just as Eva did in hers, for he would rather die than betray his Christian principles—or Cassy and Emmeline. Further, Tom dies in the act of forgiving the overseers who beat him to death, just as Christ died forgiving those who crucified him. Moreover, his death indirectly enables the freeing of the Shelby slaves, as George Shelby's decision to free them stems from his emotional response to Tom's sacrifice. The former slaveholder declares that it was on Tom's grave that he resolved never to own another slave, and that when his former slaves look at Uncle Tom's cabin, they should remember that they owe their liberty to the selfless soul of Uncle Tom. Thus the meaning of the novel's title becomes clear. The modest cabin symbolizes both the suffering of Uncle Tom and the influence of that Christ-like suffering on the conscience of George Shelby. In this way, it connects directly to two of the main themes of the novel, the evils of slavery and the effectiveness of Christianity in abolishing it.

While the reunions between George Harris and Madame de Thoux and between Cassy and Eliza may seem nothing more than an example of logic-stretching nineteenth-century sentimentalism, they do provide some literary value. While the trope of the family reunion does constitute a trite convention in much of literature, here it symbolically resolves Stowe's theme of families torn apart by slavery. The book repeatedly condemns slavery for separating parents and children, especially mothers and daughters. Now, after and partly because of Tom's death, the family is reunited.

The family's final trip to Africa touches on an issue that sparked much debate during Stowe's time. This debate centered on whether blacks should belong to a separate nation of their own, a notion that Abraham Lincoln briefly supported. Although Stowe portrays the family's move to Africa as a positive development, she vehemently emphasizes in Chapter XLV that freed slaves should not be shipped off to Africa without consideration of their individual needs and wishes. Rather, if they choose, they should be able to live in the United States and partake of an American society.

In her final chapter, Stowe articulates as an expository polemic what she has implied throughout the book in her literary narrative. While she has periodically erupted into direct addresses of her reader, now she shifts to a sustained mode of pointed persuasion. Her last paragraphs deliver a charged sermon demanding the freedom of all slaves. She notes that, although Tom's death offers salvation to many, it cannot end black oppression definitively. At the conclusion of the story, many slaves continue to live in misery under Legree. Such misery will persist, Stowe argues, until slavery is eliminated as an institution.

Important Quotations Explained

1. *"You ought to be ashamed, John! Poor, homeless, houseless creatures! It's a shameful, wicked, abominable law, and I'll break it, for one, the first time I get a chance; and I hope I shall have a chance, I do! Things have got to a pretty pass, if a woman can't give a warm supper and a bed to poor, starving creatures, just because they are slaves, and have been abused and oppressed all their lives, poor things!"* *"But, Mary, just listen to me. Your feelings are all quite right, dear . . . but, then, dear, we mustn't suffer our feelings to run away with our judgment; you must consider it's not a matter of private feeling, — there are great public interests involved, — there is a state of public agitation rising, that we must put aside our private feelings."* *"Now, John, I don't know anything about politics, but I can read my Bible; and there I see that I must feed the hungry, clothe the naked, and comfort the desolate; and that Bible I mean to follow."*

This exchange occurs in Chapter IX, between Senator Bird and his wife, just before Eliza arrives at their doorstep. The quote crystallizes some of the main themes of the novel, condemning slavery as contrary to Christianity and portraying a woman as more morally trustworthy than her male counterpart. More specifically, this passage bears witness to Stowe's attack on a common claim of her time—that slavery, and laws such as the Fugitive Slave Act, should be tolerated in the interest of greater public interest or civic order. Arguing against a law that basically paraphrases the historical Fugitive Slave Act, Mrs. Bird routs Senator Bird by insisting that she will follow her conscience and her Bible rather than an immoral law. She thus asserts that inner conscience should take precedence over law as a guide to virtue. This idea receives reiteration throughout *Uncle Tom's Cabin*. In Chapter XLV, Stowe writes, "There is only one thing that every individual can do—they can see to it that *they feel right*."

2. *"I looks like gwine to heaven," said the woman; "an't thar
    where white folks is gwine? S'pose they'd have me thar? I'd
    rather go to torment, and get away from Mas'r and Missis."*

The horribly abused slave Prue speaks these words in Chapter
XVIII, when Tom tries to convince her to find God and lead a Christian life, which he tells her will assure her an eternal reward in
heaven. With this one line, Prue dramatically illustrates the extent to
which racial politics and slavery were impressed upon slaves as
unalterable, universal facts of existence. She assumes that if white
people are going to heaven, she will be required to work as a slave to
them in the afterlife. She unwittingly offers a devastating commen-
tary on the horror of life as a slave when she says that she would
rather go to hell ("torment") to escape her master and his wife than
go to paradise with them. Stowe intended her novel for a largely
Christian audience, and with these lines she meant to shock the
reader into an awareness of the extreme misery slaves endured.

3. *"Mas'r, if you was sick, or in trouble, or dying, and I could save ye, I'd give ye my heart's blood; and, if taking every drop of blood in this poor old body would save your precious soul, I'd give 'em freely, as the Lord gave his for me. Oh, Mas'r! don't bring this great sin on your soul! It will hurt you more than't will me! Do the worst you can, my troubles'll be over soon; but, if ye don't repent, yours won't never end!"*

Tom speaks these words to Legree in Chapter XL as he pleads not to be beaten for refusing to divulge information about Cassy's escape. Tom urges Legree to reconsider, not for Tom's sake, but for Legree's. Tom explains that his own "troubles" will soon end (i.e., he will die and go to paradise), but the damage Legree does to his own soul will lead to his eternal damnation. The quote reveals the extent of Tom's piety and selflessness. Threatened with pain and death by a man who oppresses and torments him, Tom's first thought is for his oppressor's soul. He even tells Legree that he would give his "heart's blood" to save him. In these lines and elsewhere, Tom seems to prove the validity of the Christian injunction to "love thy enemy." Because he continues to love Legree, Tom ultimately defeats him, even in death.

QUOTATIONS

4.   *"Witness, eternal God! Oh, witness that, from this hour, I*
      will do what one man can to drive out this curse of slavery
      from my land!"

George Shelby makes this dramatic vow after Tom's death in Chapter XLI, when he decides to work against slavery. The quote instances Stowe's most sentimental, melodramatic style, but it also brings a note of moral conclusion to the problem of how a person should undertake to stop slavery. Men like George's father and St. Clare can see the evil of slavery but continue to tolerate and practice it. St. Clare says that he does so because there is nothing one man can do to change an entire system. But Stowe advocates acting on one's own conscience, in accordance with one's personal relationship to God. When George declares that he will do *"what one man can"* he essentially overrides all concerns about "the system." Every individual should work against oppression to the extent that he or she can, in his or her own life. If all people did this, Stowe implies, following their consciences and practicing Christian love, then slavery would cease to exist.

5. *"It was on his grave, my friends, that I resolved, before God, that I would never own another slave, while it is possible to free him; that nobody, through me, should ever run the risk of being parted from home and friends, and dying on a lonely plantation, as he died. So, when you rejoice in your freedom, think that you owe it to that good old soul, and pay it back in kindness to his wife and children. Think of your freedom, every time you see UNCLE TOM'S CABIN; and let it be a memorial to put you all in mind to follow in his steps, and be as honest and faithful and Christian as he was."*

This quotation from Chapter XLIV is George Shelby's speech to his slaves as he sets them all free, fulfilling the dramatic vow he made two chapters earlier. The speech explains the novel's title and establishes the image of Uncle Tom's cabin as the central metaphor of the novel. When George Shelby sees the house, he remembers that Uncle Tom was taken from it, separating him from his wife and children and tearing apart his family. He therefore tells his former slaves to think of their freedom when they see the cabin and to resolve to lead lives of Christian piety, following Tom's example. In this way, the cabin becomes a metaphor for the destructive power of slavery, which can split apart a family and break a home. It also comes to stand for the redemptive power of Christianity and love—for Tom's enactment of these at his death motivated Shelby to set his slaves free. Thus the cabin comes to embody two of the novel's central themes, uniting the idea of slavery's vice and Christianity's redemption in a single image.

QUOTATIONS

KEY FACTS

FULL TITLE
Uncle Tom's Cabin or, Life Among the Lowly

AUTHOR
Harriet Beecher Stowe

TYPE OF WORK
Novel

GENRE
Anti-slavery novel, novel of social protest

LANGUAGE
English

TIME AND PLACE WRITTEN
1850–1851; Brunswick, Maine

DATE OF FIRST PUBLICATION
1851

PUBLISHER
The National Era (serial publication)

NARRATOR
The narrator is sometimes omniscient—informed of the histories of the various characters unknown to other participants in the plot—and sometimes a plausible real person, reporting what he or she has perceived or experienced. In both modes, however, the narrator is far from objective and often lectures the reader.

POINT OF VIEW
The novel is told largely in the third person but often in the second. The narrative enters the minds of many of the characters but sympathizes mostly with the slaves in the book.

TONE
Stowe's attitude toward the story seems to be identical with that of the narrator.

TENSE
Past

SETTING (TIME)
Around the early 1850s

SETTING (PLACE)
The American South (Kentucky and Louisiana). Eliza and
George's escape takes them through Ohio and several Northern
Quaker settlements, then into Canada.

PROTAGONIST
Uncle Tom in the main narrative; Eliza and George Harris in the subplot

MAJOR CONFLICT
Whether practiced by kind or cruel masters, slavery injects
misery into the lives of Southern blacks, testing their courage and
their faith.

RISING ACTION
Uncle Tom comes to live under increasingly evil masters; his faith
begins to falter; while working at the Legree plantation, he
encourages Cassy and Emmeline to escape; he refuses to
compromise his values by helping Legree hunt them down

CLIMAX
The sequence of events surrounding Uncle Tom's renewal of
religious faith and his death, Chapters XXXVIII-LXI

FALLING ACTION
George Shelby's emancipation of his slaves in Chapter XLIII,
which is motivated by his witnessing Tom's death

THEMES
The evil of slavery; the incompatibility of slavery and Christian
values; the moral power of women

MOTIFS
Christ figures; idealized women; the supernatural

SYMBOLS
Uncle Tom's cabin (the destructive power of slavery and the
power of Christian love to defeat it); Eliza's leap across the Ohio
River (the transition from slavery to freedom); geography (North
represents freedom, South represents slavery and oppression)

FORESHADOWING
Eva's statement that she will soon join the angels foreshadows
her death.

STUDY QUESTIONS &
ESSAY TOPICS

STUDY QUESTIONS

1. *Discuss the differences between the portrayals of men and women in Uncle Tom's Cabin. Does Tom fit with the rest of the men in the book? Why or why not? How does the portrayal of women reveal Stowe's feminism?*

Women often take the actively moral role in *Uncle Tom's Cabin*. Often idealized as almost angelic mothers, wives, and counselors, they become guiding moral lights. Examples of such figures include Mrs. Shelby, Mrs. Bird, St. Clare's mother, and Legree's mother. In contrast, Stowe often portrays men as gruff, avaricious, and morally weaker than their female counterparts. Uncle Tom provides the one exception to this trend. Like many of the female characters, Tom serves the role of moral guide. Perhaps this parallel can be explained if one takes into account the similar position of disempowerment held by both white women and black slaves. Stowe never explicitly makes a connection between the oppression of women and the oppression of blacks, but she does imply it through her structure of parallelism and contrast.

2. *Discuss Stowe's use of opposites and the technique of contrast in Uncle Tom's Cabin.*

Parallels and contrasts lend Uncle Tom's Cabin its structure and inform its rhetorical power. The book features two opposing plots, the slave narrative and the escape narrative. One could compare the different directions, both literally and symbolically, that these plots take. Eliza and her husband travel ever farther north, finding freedom and happiness, while Tom travels ever farther south, entering into martyrdom and death.

Other contrasts in the book include that between the good mother narrative of Eliza with the bad mother narrative of Cassy. One could also compare and contrast the roles of the various women in the book, from the upright Mrs. Shelby to the appalling Marie; additionally, one could contrast the childhood innocence of Eva with the adult cynicism of Haley, Legree, or St. Clare. Uncle Tom's passive martyrdom contrasts with, but does not oppose, George Harris's active heroism. This use of contrast seems particularly apt for a book that critiques a politically divided nation and a society organized by differences of skin color and gender. Against the grain of conventional thinking, the text imposes its own similarities and differences that cut across received categories. The text compares the subjugated positions of blacks and white women, links Tom and the Quakers in their religiosity, associates Eva with Topsy in their otherworldly energy and naiveté, and connects both Tom and Eva with Jesus Christ. Simon Legree, the representative of slavery's most horrendous evils, was born in the North, in Vermont. On the other hand, George Shelby, who eventually sets his slaves free, lives his whole life on a Southern plantation. With these associations Stowe challenges conventional dichotomies between black and white, male and female, and North and South.

3. *What roles do circumstance and chance play in Uncle
Tom's Cabin? Does the text use either of them to help
explain the existence of slavery?*

Stowe acknowledges that circumstances of geography and birth
may decide whether a person practices slavery, but she does not
allow circumstance or chance to excuse these people. For instance,
St. Clare tells Miss Ophelia that many of the prominent people in
New England would be prominent slaveholders if they lived in the
South. However, Stowe does not allow this to serve as a justification
of slavery but rather as an indictment against humanity. All people
possess some measure of evil, and therefore all people are capable of
the evil of owning slaves. Depending on the circumstances of one's
birth, the evil in one's life takes different forms. One should work
toward eradicating the circumstances that allow this evil to become
institutionalized.

SUGGESTED ESSAY TOPICS

1. *In what ways does Stowe present the incompatibility of slavery with the Christian ethic of love and tolerance? How do the novel's Christ figures underscore its basic Christian messages?*

2. *Compare and contrast Tom's three owners in the novel — Shelby, St. Clare, and Legree. How are they alike? How are they different? Do they appear in the novel according to any particular sequence, and if so, how does this progression relate to the general themes of the book?*

3. *Discuss the role of Eva in the novel. In what ways does she contribute to the novel's larger messages?*

4. *How do Stowe's political objectives affect the style and formal aspects of the novel? In designing her characters to make a point, did she make them too simple? Do the noble politics of the novel justify its literary shortcomings?*

Review & Resources

Quiz

1.   To whom does Shelby sell Tom and Harry?

     A.   Haley
     B.   Legree
     C.   St. Clare
     D.   Marie

2.   In what year was the Fugitive Slave Act passed?

     A.   1784
     B.   1841
     C.   1850
     D.   1857

3.   In what city do the St. Clares live?

     A.   Memphis
     B.   New Orleans
     C.   Louisville
     D.   Atlanta

4.   How old is Emmeline?

     A.   Ten
     B.   Thirteen
     C.   Seventeen
     D.   Fifteen

5.   Who is Eliza's mother?

     A.   Cassy
     B.   Mrs. Shelby
     C.   Mrs. Legree
     D.   Aunt Chloe

6. How many children does Uncle Tom have?

    A. One
    B. Seven
    C. Five
    D. Three

7. In what state is the Shelby farm located?

    A. Tennessee
    B. Kentucky
    C. Alabama
    D. Mississippi

8. Where does Tom first meet Eva?

    A. In New Orleans
    B. On a ferry
    C. In Memphis
    D. On a riverboat

9. In what state was Uncle Tom's Cabin written?

    A. Maine
    B. Massachusetts
    C. Georgia
    D. Ohio

10. Over what river does Eliza make her miraculous crossing?

    A. The Mississippi
    B. The Colorado
    C. The Ohio
    D. The Danube

11. Who inherits ownership of Tom when St. Clare dies?

    A. Eva
    B. Marie
    C. George Shelby
    D. Haley

12. How does St. Clare die?

    A. He drowns
    B. He suffers a heart attack
    C. He falls from a hot-air balloon
    D. He is stabbed

13. Who saves Eva from drowning?

    A. Tom
    B. Chloe
    C. George
    D. Loker

14. In what state is Legree's plantation located?

    A. Georgia
    B. Florida
    C. Louisiana
    D. Vermont

15. Who shoots Tom Loker?

    A. Eliza
    B. George Harris
    C. Harry
    D. Uncle Tom

16. Who heals Loker?

    A. Eliza
    B. Marie
    C. George Harris
    D. The Quakers

17. What term describes Cassy's racial heritage?

    A. Quadroon
    B. Mulatto
    C. Octoroon
    D. Hectoroon

REVIEW & RESOURCES

18. What President reportedly claimed that Uncle Tom's Cabin started the Civil War?

    A. Grant
    B. McKinley
    C. Lincoln
    D. Buchanan

19. From where does Eliza cross into Canada?

    A. Lake Erie
    B. Lake Huron
    C. Niagara Falls
    D. Northern Minnesota

20. Whom does St. Clare give to Ophelia to educate?

    A. Eva
    B. Prue
    C. Emmeline
    D. Topsy

21. Which character directly opposes the Fugitive Slave Law?

    A. Senator Bird
    B. Mrs. Bird
    C. St. Clare
    D. Haley

22. Who beats Uncle Tom to death?

    A. Legree
    B. St. Clare
    C. Legree's overseers
    D. George Shelby

23. What is Mrs. Shelby's first name?

    A. Emily
    B. Rachel
    C. Margaret
    D. Danielle

24. In what state does Tom die?

    A. Kentucky
    B. Tennessee
    C. Ohio
    D. Louisiana

25. To which country do George and Eliza plan to immigrate?

    A. Liberia
    B. Nigeria
    C. France
    D. Algeria

SUGGESTIONS FOR FURTHER READING

ADAMS, JOHN R. *Harriet Beecher Stowe*. Boston: Twayne Publishers, 1989.

BLOOM, HAROLD. *Harriet Beecher Stowe's* Uncle Tom's Cabin. New York: Chelsea House Publishers, 1999.

HEDRICK, JOAN D. *Harriet Beecher Stowe: a Life*. New York: Oxford University Press, 1994.

KING, WILMA, et al. *Toward the Promised Land: From* Uncle Tom's Cabin *to the Onset of the Civil War (1851-1861)*. New York: Chelsea House Publishers, 1995.

KIRKHAM, E. BRUCE. *The Building of* Uncle Tom's Cabin. Knoxville: University of Tennessee Press, 1977.

LOWANCE, MASON I., et. al., ed. *The Stowe Debate: Rhetorical Strategies in* Uncle Tom's Cabin. Amherst: University of Massachusetts Press, 1994.

STOWE, HARRIET BEECHER. *A Key to* Uncle Tom's Cabin: *Presenting the Original Facts and Documents upon Which the Story is Founded*. New York: Applewood Books, 1998.

SPARKNOTES
TEST PREPARATION
GUIDES

The SparkNotes team figured it was time to cut standardized tests down to size. We've studied the tests for you, so that SparkNotes test prep guides are:

Smarter
Packed with critical-thinking skills and test-taking strategies that will improve your score.

Better
Fully up to date, covering all new features of the tests, with study tips on every type of question.

Faster
Our books cover exactly what you need to know for the test. No more, no less.

SPARKNOTES™ LITERATURE GUIDES

1984
The Adventures of
Huckleberry Finn
The Adventures of Tom
Sawyer
The Aeneid
All Quiet on the
Western Front
And Then There Were
None
Angela's Ashes
Animal Farm
Anna Karenina
Anne of Green Gables
Anthem
Antony and Cleopatra
Aristotle's Ethics
As I Lay Dying
As You Like It
Atlas Shrugged
The Awakening
The Autobiography of
Malcolm X
The Bean Trees
The Bell Jar
Beloved
Beowulf
Billy Budd
Black Boy
Bless Me, Ultima
The Bluest Eye
Brave New World
The Brothers
Karamazov
The Call of the Wild
Candide
The Canterbury Tales
Catch-22
The Catcher in the Rye
The Chocolate War
The Chosen
Cold Mountain
Cold Sassy Tree
The Color Purple
The Count of Monte
Cristo
Crime and Punishment
The Crucible
Cry, the Beloved
Country
Cyrano de Bergerac
David Copperfield

Death of a Salesman
The Death of Socrates
The Diary of a Young
Girl
A Doll's House
Don Quixote
Dr. Faustus
Dr. Jekyll and Mr. Hyde
Dracula
Dune
East of Eden
Edith Hamilton's
Mythology
Emma
Ethan Frome
Fahrenheit 451
Fallen Angels
A Farewell to Arms
Farewell to Manzanar
Flowers for Algernon
For Whom the Bell
Tolls
The Fountainhead
Frankenstein
The Giver
The Glass Menagerie
Gone With the Wind
The Good Earth
The Grapes of Wrath
Great Expectations
The Great Gatsby
Greek Classics
Grendel
Gulliver's Travels
Hamlet
The Handmaid's Tale
Hard Times
Harry Potter and the
Sorcerer's Stone
Heart of Darkness
Henry IV, Part I
Henry V
Hiroshima
The Hobbit
The House of Seven
Gables
I Know Why the Caged
Bird Sings
The Iliad
Inferno
Inherit the Wind
Invisible Man

Jane Eyre
Johnny Tremain
The Joy Luck Club
Julius Caesar
The Jungle
The Killer Angels
King Lear
The Last of the
Mohicans
Les Miserables
A Lesson Before Dying
The Little Prince
Little Women
Lord of the Flies
The Lord of the Rings
Macbeth
Madame Bovary
A Man for All Seasons
The Mayor of
Casterbridge
The Merchant of Venice
A Midsummer Night's
Dream
Moby Dick
Much Ado About
Nothing
My Antonia
Narrative of the Life of
Frederick Douglass
Native Son
The New Testament
Night
Notes from
Underground
The Odyssey
The Oedipus Plays
Of Mice and Men
The Old Man and the
Sea
The Old Testament
Oliver Twist
The Once and Future
King
One Day in the Life of
Ivan Denisovich
One Flew Over the
Cuckoo's Nest
One Hundred Years of
Solitude
Othello
Our Town
The Outsiders

Paradise Lost
A Passage to India
The Pearl
The Picture of Dorian
Gray
Poe's Short Stories
A Portrait of the Artist
as a Young Man
Pride and Prejudice
The Prince
A Raisin in the Sun
The Red Badge of
Courage
The Republic
Richard III
Robinson Crusoe
Romeo and Juliet
The Scarlet Letter
A Separate Peace
Silas Marner
Sir Gawain and the
Green Knight
Slaughterhouse-Five
Snow Falling on Cedars
Song of Solomon
The Sound and the Fury
Steppenwolf
The Stranger
Streetcar Named
Desire
The Sun Also Rises
A Tale of Two Cities
The Taming of the
Shrew
The Tempest
Tess of the d'Ubervilles
Their Eyes Were
Watching God
Things Fall Apart
The Things They
Carried
To Kill a Mockingbird
To the Lighthouse
Treasure Island
Twelfth Night
Ulysses
Uncle Tom's Cabin
Walden
War and Peace
Wuthering Heights
A Yellow Raft in Blue
Water